A Theurgist's
BOOK OF HOURS

A Theurgist's
Book of Hours

Jeffrey S. Kupperman

PUBLISHED BY AVALONIA
WWW.AVALONIABOOKS.COM

PUBLISHED BY AVALONIA

BM AVALONIA
LONDON
WC1N 3XX
ENGLAND, UK

WWW.AVALONIABOOKS.COM

A THEURGIST'S BOOK OF HOURS
COPYRIGHT © JEFFREY S. KUPPERMAN 2021

ISBN: 978-1-905297-89-4

FIRST EDITION, MAY 2021

DESIGN BY მელია

COVER ART: JEFFREY S. KUPPERMAN

ILLUSTRATIONS BY JEFFREY S. KUPPERMAN

BRITISH LIBRARY CATALOGUING IN PUBLICATION DATA. A CATALOGUE RECORD FOR THIS BOOK IS AVAILABLE FROM THE BRITISH LIBRARY.

Dedication

To the Great Gods and the Series of the Greater Kinds

About the Author

Jeffrey S. Kupperman has studied Neoplatonism, Hermetics, Kabbalah, and the Western Mystery Tradition for more than 25 years and is a hierarch of the Ekklesia Neoplatonismos Theourgia. He is the author of Living Theurgy (Avalonia, 2014) and the founder and publisher of the Journal of the Western Mystery Tradition (jwmt.org). Jeffrey lives in the Midwest USA where he teaches philosophy and religious studies, graphic designs, researches, writes, paints, and raises his children. Not necessarily in that order.

Table of Contents

MONTHLY HIEROMENIAS
CHAPTER 7 PRAYER SERVICES FOR THE MONTHS

THEORIA

Part I: Theoria

Introduction

A Theurgist's Book of Hours is part of an effort to bring late Neoplatonic thought, what might be called 'religious Neoplatonism,' and practice into the modern world and to introduce it to those who may benefit from such a praxis. In some ways, this may be seen as a sequel to *Living Theurgy*.[1] However, *A Theurgist's Book of Hours* is not dependent upon any previous text. Instead, this book is designed to be accessible to anyone, regardless of their experience with, or knowledge of, late Neoplatonism.

All of this, however, brings up three important questions. The first of these is "what is Neoplatonism?" Neoplatonism, sometimes also Neo-Platonism, is a term coined by 19th century German scholars to describe a number of related schools of Platonic thought starting with the Egyptian Plotinus in the first quarter of the third century C.E.. So-called 'late Neoplatonism' begins in Neoplatonism's third generation, with the Syrian Platonist Iamblichus. Iamblichus is a student of a student of Plotinus, Porphyry of Tyre, and much of his extant writing career is marked by his disagreements with his teacher. Perhaps most importantly, Iamblichus is responsible for bringing the practice of theurgy into Neoplatonic practice. For the most part, this book engages in an Iamblichean form of Neoplatonism.

Second: "what is 'theurgy'?" The Anglicized word 'theurgy' comes from the Greek *theourgia*. The first part of the word means 'god,' the second is derived from a word meaning 'activity.' Often, theurgy is described as 'god working.' More formally, theurgy is the engagement in ritual activities in imitation and participation of a god, God, or other divine being. Through theurgy the practitioner, or theurgist, engages in a process of divinization and demiurgy. Divinization is to become like God or the gods, so far as possible. Demiurgy is engaging in divine creative activity in the realm of generation, which is to say here, the universe all around us. Neoplatonic theurgic practice, which has antecedents in middle Platonic Hermetism, is eventually brought into

---

[1] *Avalonia Books, 2014.*

mainstream Christianity through the writings of the early 6th-century theologian now known as pseudo-Dionysius.[2] It is also found in Jewish mystical writings, especially those of Rabbi Moshe Cordovero, and various forms of Sufism. It is arguably one of the foundations of Western esoteric practice.

Third: "what is a 'Book of Hours'?" Books of Hours were introduced to medieval Christianity as a way for people, especially the wealthy, to engage in some monastic practices without joining a monastery. They often contain seven or eight sections, including the Liturgy of the Hours, a liturgical calendar and several different Psalms.

How is this at all related to a Neoplatonic Book of Hours? Neoplatonism itself, though of Hellenic pagan origins, can transcend any particular religiosity. It is instead what may be described as a hermeneutic or interpretive lens through which various religious and philosophical practices can be viewed and engaged. That is to say, we are here borrowing from Christianity, much as Christianity, especially in its Orthodox form, has often borrowed from Neoplatonism.

The idea of a Neoplatonic Book of Hours is not original. The idea is first introduced by Gemistus Pletho, one of the men, along with Cosimo de'Medici and Marsilio Ficino, who was responsible for the birth of Renaissance Neoplatonism. Pletho, or Plethon, is a 14th century Greek Platonist. Although originally an Orthodox Christian, Plethon comes to embrace a form of Hellenic, pagan, Neoplatonism, though one with many Orthodox overtones. In his attempt to revive Hellenic polytheism, Plethon writes the *Nomoi*, of which only fragments now remain.[3] An important part of the *Nomoi* is a liturgical calendar for prayer practice. This includes the singing of hymns, the recitations of prayers, and philosophical discussions, or at least the reading of Plato and relevant commentaries.

---

[2] There are also theurgic elements in some Gnostic Christian practices before this.
[3] See chapter two.

CHAPTER 1

A Theory of Prayer

What is prayer? What does it do? What does it have to do with theurgy? Prayer is a traditional part of many religions. However, different religions define prayer differently. The general benefits of prayer, when approached theurgically, are enormous. In brief, prayer nurtures the mind, makes us more receptive to divine beings, habituates us to the otherwise potentially lethal divine light, perfects our ability to contact the gods, uplifts our minds to those of the gods, links us to them, purifies our pneumatic vehicle, brings out the divine element in the human soul, and makes us "the familiar consorts of the gods."[4] Prayer is so important that "no sacred act can take place"[5] without it.

Iamblichus's Theory of Prayer

Iamblichus discusses theurgic prayer in the beginning of the fifth chapter of his theurgic magnum opus *De Mysteriis*. It is through prayer that "an indissoluble hieratic communion is created with the gods."[6] Iamblichus sets out three levels of prayer: introductory, conjunctive, and ineffable unification. These are based on the Chaldean Oracles, about which Iamblichus writes a twenty-eight or more volume treatise,[7] all of which have since been lost. The first level makes contact with the gods, or potentially any of the beings referred to as the 'greater kinds' beneath them. This includes archangels, angels, daimons, heroes, and purified (human) souls. At this level of prayer,

---

[4] DM V.26, 277
[5] Ibid.
[6] Ibid., 275.
[7] Dillon, Iamblichi, 24.

acquaintance and friendship with divine beings are made. Here, knowledge of the gods, and awareness of their presence, is achieved.[8]

Conjunction produces a union between the theurgist and the divine being to whom prayer is offered. This level also brings about divine blessings in the forms of divine illumination, what might be described as magical works or the 'common achievement of projects,'[9] and finally the perfection of the soul through immaterial fire. Here the gifts of the gods, which Iamblichus describes throughout the second chapter of *De Mysteriis*,[10] are made manifest.

When writing *De Mysteriis* in response to his former teacher's questions about theurgy, Iamblichus had not yet entered his 'Chaldean phase,' where he codifies the entire Chaldean system along Platonic lines. However, there appears to be a direct connection between the system of the *Chaldean Oracles* and this level of prayer. In the Chaldean system, as set out in what remains of the second century C.E. *Chaldean Oracles*, conjunction is a kind of invocatory prayer or ritual. It is through conjunction that Julian the Theurgist, the author, or transmitter, of the *Oracles*, is conjoined with the soul of Plato and "all the gods."[11] Conjunction involves the use of divine names, the famous *voces mysticae* or *nomina barbara*. These names, though unintelligible to us, are understood by theurgists to have meaning to the gods and act as their symbols and tokens in the realm of generation. Such names are rhythmically chanted either by themselves or, as seen in the *Papyri Graecae Magicae*, as part of larger prayers.[12]

The final level, ineffable unification, brings about noetic union with the gods.[13] Such a union is beyond comprehension, and possibly even beyond conscious human experience, establishing the theurgist completely in the god. This level is likely to be related to the Chaldean rites of 'binding and loosing.' These rites bind a theurgist to a divine being in a form of divine possession. Unlike the level of conjunction, where the focus is upon the theurgist, at this level it is upon the god, who has control over the process.[14] This means that despite the language of control inherent

---

8 Dillon, *Iamblichi*, 408.
9 DM V.26, 275.
10 Specifically, DM II.3-9, 87-107.
11 Majercik, *Oracles*, 25.
12 Ibid., 25-6.
13 Ibid., 275-7.
14 Majercik, *Oracles*, 27.

in the name of this kind of rite, the gods are in no way coerced by the theurgist, nor can they be, due to their ontological superiority over humanity, a point Iamblichus makes several times. This idea is strongly hinted at in the *Oracles* themselves:

> *"I [Hekate] have come, Hearkening to your very eloquent prayer, which the nature of mortals has discovered at the suggestion of the gods."*[15]

This suggests the gods bestow their munificence due to their 'friendship' with the theurgist. By this is meant that by becoming so similar to the gods they hymn the theurgist deeply participates the gods, and by doing so gains access to their blessings and perfection.[16] Without the gods' active participation, this level of prayer is impossible to achieve, as is true of all theurgy.

Proclus' Theory of Prayer

Proclus' theory of prayer, which appears in his *Timaeus* commentary, is an elaboration of Iamblichus'. In this commentary Proclus hopes to both describe Iamblichus' theory and make it fit into Platonic thought. Considering that Iamblichus' presentation of prayer is of Platonised Chaldean origin rather than simply Platonism, it is difficult to say how successful Proclus might be at his second goal. In achieving his first goal, Proclus sets out a somewhat modified version of Iamblichus' theory, extrapolating the three phases of prayer into five.[17]

The first of Proclus' five stages of prayer is *gnosis*, or knowledge of the divinities to which the prayers are addressed. Second, the theurgist becomes familiar with the divinities, becoming more like them, becoming more pure, chaste, educated, and ordered. Contact with the divine is next, linking the highest part of the rational soul with the divinity. Fourth, the divinity is approached, which uses language borrowed from the *Chaldean Oracles*. The complete fragment, found in Proclus' *Timaeus* commentary, reads:

---

[15] *CO, fr. 222.*
[16] *C.f. Van Den Berg, Hymns, 87.*
[17] *Van Den Berg, Hymns, 88-9.*

> *In addition to these things, there is the 'approaching' — for the oracle calls it thus:*
> *"For the mortal who has approached the fire will possess the light from God."*
> *(The 'approaching') allows us a greater communion and a more distinct participation in the light of*
> *the gods.*[18]

The final level is *henosis*; the unification of the theurgist with the divinity. This has the effect of establishing the One or highest divine principle of the soul with the One of the gods. In doing this the theurgist's *energeiai*, activities, become one with those of the gods. In this demarcation of the stages of prayer, phases one and two correlate to Iamblichus' first stage, stages three and four to his second level and Proclus' fifth is nearly identical to Iamblichus' third.

If Iamblichus wrote any hymns, none have survived. However, at least five of Proclus' have.[19] These hymns show that not all levels of prayer are necessarily present in any one hymn. For instance, the hymn to Helios focuses on the fourth level. The two hymns to Aphrodite focus on the second level. None of the extant prayers rise to the final level. This may be because the final level of *henosis* is only for the henads, the gods at the highest level of the noetic, or intelligible, realm and the gods of the surviving hymns are leader gods, functioning much farther down in the divine hierarchy.

Although Proclus' highest level of prayer is reserved for the highest level of gods, this may not hold true for Iamblichus. Most of what is known of Iamblichus' prayer theory comes from *De Mysteriis*. *De Mysteriis* is primarily about material theurgy and accessing the visible gods, or the gods embodied by the heavenly spheres. The activity of these gods is much farther down than that of the henads, focusing on the realm of generation rather than the intelligible. Also, the *nomina barbara* are absent from Proclus' prayers. This is, once again, due to the level of gods being contacted. Iamblichus description of prayer in DM V.26 makes no mention of these names in any way. However, elsewhere it is clear the *nomina barbara* are an important part of his theurgic prayer practice.[20] Concerning these, Iamblichus follows the injunction of the *Chaldean Oracles*: "Do not

---

[18] *CO, fr. 121.*
[19] *Possibly six. Some have suggested that the Homeric hymn to Ares is a product of Proclus'.*
[20] *C.f. DM VII.5, 299.*

change the *nomina barbara*."[21] This is because they are understood to come directly from the gods and act as their symbols and tokens in the material world.

Not an explicit part of either Iamblichus' or Proclus' theory of prayer, but otherwise clear from their other writings, is that the work of theurgic prayer, and that of theurgists in general, is at least two-fold. Most obviously is the effect of prayer on the worshipper. On this, these theories are relatively clear. Less clear, however, is the idea that theurgic work is not only for the benefit of the individual but for every human soul.

That there is a group connotation to the overall effect of prayer can be seen, for instance, quite explicitly in Iamblichus. In his *Philebus* commentary, for instance, Proclus writes:

> *Why is it upon the mixed life that the Cause bestows itself? Because as being all things it has an affinity with that which is all-embracing. For that which is simple is not capable of receiving the power of the Cause, which ineffably, transcending unity, embraces all things. For this reason the divine Iamblichus declares that it is impossible to partake as an individual of the universal orders, but only in communion with the divine choir of those who, with minds united, experience a common uplift.*[22]

However, this is not enough. The theurgist's work is not just for their own benefit, or the benefit of those others with whom she works but, like the philosopher queens and kings of Plato's *Republic*, their work is not done until all are raised.[23]

Tokens and Symbols

Theurgic hymns, the hymns with which we are primarily concerned, are symbol-laden. These symbols are not of the mundane sort, such as the metaphors of a love poem. Instead, they are what are known as *sunthemata*, tokens or signatures, and *symbola*, symbols. *Sunthemata* and *symbola* are divine in their origin, coming from the primary creative principles called *Demiurgoi*, Demiurges, craftsmen or creators, and the highest levels of divine beings.

---

[21] CO, fr. 150.
[22] In Phileb., fr. 6.
[23] C.f. Kupperman, Living Theurgy, 64, 66-8.

D.M. Van Den Berg, in his translation and analysis of Proclus' surviving hymns, identifies four kinds of symbols that can be employed in theurgic prayer.[24] Changing Van Den Berg's ordering, we have:

- *symbolic names*
- *innate symbols*
- *symbolic myths*
- *material symbols.*

Each has several sub-groups and is found, to varying degrees, in Proclus' myths, but also in other extant Neoplatonic hymns, such as those of Synesius, the 5th century Bishop of Ptolemais, and student of the pagan Neoplatonist Hypatia.

Symbolic Names

Symbolic names are expressed in two ways. The first, though absent from Proclus' hymns, are the *nomina barbara*. These divine names consist of long strings of generally unintelligible vowels and consonants. Occasionally we can discern an altered form of the name of an Egyptian deity in the *nomina*, and there is a definite pattern to be found in many of the names, but for the most part the names appear to have no definite meaning. At least not to us. Iamblichus tells us the divine names do have meaning, but being of divine origin, their meaning is only accessible to the gods to whom they belong.[25]

Such names may be described as inherently symbolic. Coming directly from the gods, the *nomina barbara* contain not only their thoughts and essences but the gods themselves. The names are not, in and of themselves, the gods, nor are they pieces of the gods, and this is true of all *sunthemata* and *symbola*. However, they are so closely related to the gods that the gods are said to be present in their names.[26] Again, this is ultimately true for all *sunthemata*. However the divine names, particularly in this form, and even if they are related to material theurgy, are a part of a

---

24 Van Den Berg, Hymns, 91-107.
25 DM VII.4, 297-9.
26 Uždavinys, Theurgy, 133.

form of theurgy higher than most people would practice: immaterial theurgy.[27] As such, their theurgic value cannot be underestimated as they are able to effect a connection with the gods at a higher level than material symbols.

Symbolic names can also take the form of more mundane appellations. The common names of the gods are themselves of this variety, and even these may have hidden meanings - at least that is how the later Platonists read Plato's *Cratylus*. This dialogue presents folk etymologies of several divine names, including Kronos, who, due to the rendering of his name, takes on the role of the divine intellect, the celestial Demiurgos.[28] These are the kinds of names and titles found in Proclus' hymns as well as the hymns and prayers contained herein.

Innate Symbols

Innate symbols are more difficult, and will not be found explicitly spelt out in a hymn. An innate symbol is one that is, because of its very nature, symbolic of something else. Unlike symbols where a connection is inferred or learned, innate symbols are symbolic of something simply because of what they are. For instance, Proclus is originally from Byzantium. Traditionally, Byzantium is dedicated to Athena. Because of this, Proclus is able to say that he belongs to Athena. His place of birth is symbolic of Athena and his birth there connects him to her. Both the city and Proclus belong to her.[29] The rays of the sun are inherently symbolic of Helios, the sun god. Those born of Lycia are connected to Aphrodite,[30] and so on. The idea of places being sacred to particular divinities is not unique to the Greeks. For instance, the Enochian system of Dr. John Dee and Edward Kelley placed different spirits over different parts of the world and Judaism places 70 angels over the nations of the world.

---

[27] Shaw, "Geometry," 124.
[28] Crat. 396b.
[29] Van Den Berg, Hymns, 91.
[30] Ibid., 91-2.

Symbolic Myths

Plato rejects the myths of Homer and Hessiod as irreligious and blasphemous. To Plato, they represent the gods as little more than divinized humans, filled with anger, lust, and other human detritus. For Plato, the gods are perfect and beyond any sort of human conception, and certainly beyond, and above, human behaviour. However, the later Platonists do not follow Plato on this, and instead re-interpret such stories as philosophical symbols, specifically using the word *symbolon*, a symbol, rather than *allegoria* or *hyponoia*.[31]

Most often, when found in hymns, symbolic myths are not a complete retelling of any particular story. Instead, they most commonly appear as brief references to a story, maybe via a title, or a turn of phrase. These may be described as 'non-narrative' myths, or elements of some mythic narrative distilled into a description that is evocative of the story from which it comes.[32] The use of such myths is only possible because the stories themselves, though possibly altered by humans, originate with the gods. Such myths are used by inspired poets, philosophers, and the gods themselves through their oracles.[33] An example of this can be seen in fragment 189 of the *Chaldean Oracles*, which describes Hecate, who is described in stories as having three faces, as having "faces on all sides."

Material Symbols

Material symbols are, today, possibly the most well recognized symbolic form. What else are a crucifix, a Bishop's crosier, or the mitre-topped sceptre of the Hegemon but material symbols? The crucifix brings to mind the death and resurrection of Christ, the crosier is symbolic of the Bishop's role as shepherd of their congregation, which again reflects New Testament language. In the neophyte initiation ritual of the Order of the Golden Dawn, we are told the Hegemon's sceptre represents religion.[34]

---

31 Ibid. 93.
32 Kupperman, "Where the Goddess and Gold Walk, "174-6.
33 Sallustius, Gods, III.
34 Regardie, Golden Dawn, 119.

In general, material symbols are forms of *sunthemata*. Most often, *sunthemata* are approached from the natural world. In his *On the Sacrificial Art*, Proclus lists the heliotrope, lotus, sunstone, rooster, and lion as being tokens of the sun and its deity.[35] These are all natural things. A crucifix, a crosier, a talisman, are not. Nevertheless, they are symbolic tools representing a higher reality, such as Christ or the visible, planetary gods and their movement. Much as with innate symbols, entire regions, such as the whole of Athens, sacred to Athena, can serve as material symbols.[36] In terms of theurgic hymns, we may see such symbols employed simply by mentioning them. This brings to mind everything the symbol represents and calls upon the divine activity behind it. In theurgic ritual, however, some such symbols can also be directly employed.

Prayers

The above discusses the theories behind theurgic prayer. Theurgic prayer lets us know the gods, participate in their blessings, and ultimately become one with them. Prayer does this through the use of symbols. Such symbols may be of physical, or literary, nature, but ultimately descend from the divine realm. If this were not the case they would be useless as theurgic tools. This does not, however, tell us how to pray. Of course, there is not one particular way to pray. However, theurgic prayers, at least those developed by Proclus, tend to follow a particular format: invocation, aretology, prayer or petition.

The invocation calls upon the deity and any beings under their rule, or within their 'orbit' or 'series,' to use Neoplatonic language, which may be relevant to the prayer. In one of Proclus' hymns to Aphrodite, both Aphrodite and the Erotes who serve her are called upon. The aretology is biographical in nature. Here the hymnist recalls elements of the deity's life relevant to the prayer. For instance, we may remember Moses being placed in the Nile or the baby Hercules killing the serpents in a prayer for the protection of our children to God or Zeus. The final part is the petition, where what the theurgist wants is named. Although this may be put in the language of asking, as humility is important when standing before the divine, the Neoplatonists did not consider the gods to be passable. That is, they could not be swayed by emotion or begging. The

---

[35] Proclus, "Priestly Arts," in Copenhaver, "Hermes Trismegistus, Proclus, and a Philosophy of Magic," 104.
[36] Van Den Berg, *Hymns*, 106-7.

second part of Iamblichus' theory of prayer, where we receive the gifts of the gods and the 'common achievement of projects' comes about through the effect of the prayer on the theurgist, not the god.

Greek prayers were often written in iambic hexameter, which is the meter used by Homer and in the Homeric hymns. These particular hymns are called 'Homeric' not because they were written by Homer, but because they were written in the meter he made famous. English, however, does not work well in this meter. Thomas Taylor, the famous 18th-19th century Neoplatonist translated such poems into iambic pentameter, a meter many of us know through the works of William Shakespeare. There are also a number of meters common to English-language hymns which, if you plan to write your own hymns, are available for experimentation. The original hymns in this book are all written in 8.7.8.7D, the same meter used for Amazing Grace. The prayers are not written in meter. Instead, each consists of nine lines, divided between three different parts of the format discussed above.

CHAPTER 2

Plethon's Calendar Reform and the Theurgic Calendar

Gemistus Plethon's 14th century, neo-pagan, Neoplatonic calendar reform[37] forms one of the bases of this Book of Hours. The basic luni-solar outline of Plethon's calendar forms the foundation for this work, as does the division of the day into prayer times, and the general outline of his liturgical format. However, Plethon's hymns are not used. Also, the prayer cycle described here is somewhat more complex than Plethon's, as it engages with the movement of time and seasons rather deeper than simply associating each month with a particular deity. And, although Neoplatonic, this Book of Hours is not necessarily pagan in focus; the divine figures from a number of religions and cultures find their way into the hymns presented here. What follows is not *the* way of practice, but simply a way. For those comfortable doing so, it may be used verbatim. For those not comfortable, it may serve as a general guide to this kind of practice within a Neoplatonic context.

Plethon's Calendar

Plethon's calendrical reform is quite complex. The days of the four full weeks are numbered from 1-7, from 7-2, from 1-7, and from 7-2 again, with a final 29th and possible 30th day at the end, depending on the length of the lunar month. In this way the calendar counts up and down

---

37 Almost all the important discussion of the Nomoi fragments in relation to Plethon's calendar are found in two papers: Anastos, "Calendar," 1948 and Gandz, "Calendar-Reform," 1950. The following discussion, and in many ways the format of this entire book, is heavily indebted to these two papers.

between holidays, *hieromenias,* the sacred times of the moon or month, which fall on the first, eighth, fifteenth, twenty-second, twenty-ninth, and possibly thirtieth, days of the month.[38] These holidays or vigil days are the touchstones of each month, and each starts the midnight after the beginning of the new, first quarter, full, and third-quarter moons, with the month beginning on the midnight after the new moon.

Unlike our modern calendar, not all the days of the month are named. The first day of the month is called *noumenia,* which simply means 'new moon.' The fifteenth day is called *dichomenia,* meaning the moon at the first quarter or the 'split' or middle of the month. The last two or three days of the lunar month were also given names. The last day of the month, which may be either the 29th or 30th day, is called *hene kai nea,* "the day of the old and new [moon]." On months of 29 days, called *koilos* or "hollow" months, *hene kai nea* is the day after the 28th day, which is called *deutera tou menos phthinontos,* the "second of the descending month" or "moon." However, in a *pleres* or 'full' month, the day before *hene kai nea* is called *hene,* "the old day" or "the day of the old moon." Only full months have this extra day or *hene.*[39] The day begins at midnight, and *noumenia* explicitly begins 'with the first midnight after the conjunction of the two divinities [i.e. the sun and moon].'[40] Other days are only indicated by number, rather than name. Plethon did not name the months, but he did dedicate each one to a deity or group of deities. In order, these are Zeus, Poseidon, Hera, the Olympians, Apollo, Artemis, the gods of the sky, Athena, Dionysus, the Titans, Hephaestus, the Daimons, and the embolismic month to all the gods.

Besides 29 and 30 day months, the lengths of which are determined by the length of the lunar month at hand, Plethon included an embolismic month. This occasional, extra thirteenth month is necessary to keep the combined lunar and solar calendars synchronized over time. This additional month is necessary because of the difference between the length of a lunar and solar month. Over the years the two systems will become widely disparate. We see this in the case of Islam, which uses a purely lunar calendar. This is why we see the celebration of the holy month of Ramadan appearing at different times of the year. This is different from the Jewish calendar,

---

38 *Anastos, "Calendar," 219.*
39 *See Anastos, "Calendar," 218-19 and Gandz, "Reform," 202-3, 206, 208.*
40 *Gandz, "Reform," 202.*

which is luni-solar in nature, and so we see the holidays falling around the same time on our solar-based calendar, within a few weeks, every year.

Although we cannot be certain, Milton Anastos makes a good case for Plethon using a system to determine when to include the extra month similar to one developed by Hipparchus, who lived in the second and first centuries B.C.E.. This system intercalates a thirteenth month seven times per 19 years, or every two to three years. This allows for 235 lunations, complete lunar months, every 19 years.[41]

Although it is clear Plethon calculated his months based on the lunar cycle, it is unclear as to how he determined the beginning of the year. Anastos insists Plethon began the year on the first new moon after the winter solstice.[42] Solomon Gandz disagrees, citing Plethon's own words: "[We prescribe] the use of the natural month and year, reckoning the month according to the moon and the year according to the sun."[43] If the year is reckoned with the sun, then presumably it cannot begin according to the new moon. Instead, Gandz suggests Plethon begins the year on the winter solstice. This makes the beginning of the year land in the middle of the 12th or 13th month.[44]

Gandz comes to this conclusion based on an interpretation of Plethon saying the beginning of the year is calculated according to the solstices, beginning "with the winter solstice, when the sun, having departed farthest from us, sets out again on its way back... The first month of the year is that which is immediately preceded by the conjunction after the winter solstice etc."[45] Gandz says this must mean the year starts on the winter solstice itself. Otherwise, Plethon would be waiting until the next new moon to start the year, forcing the sun to bow to the moon, which Plethon, Gandz says, would not do.[46] However, it is still true that if the first month of the new year begins on the new moon after the winter solstice, it is the winter solstice that determines the beginning of the new year.

---

41 Anastos, "Calendar," 201.
42 Ibid., 206-13.
43 Gandz, "Reform," 202.
44 Ibid., 204.
45 Ibid.
46 Ibid.

The difference between Anastos and Gandz is that for Anastos the new year also begins with the new month following the winter solstice,[47] whereas for Gandz it begins in the middle of the lunar month. In either case, the winter solstice functions as an anchor for the lunar calendar. It is a time that can be calculated accurately, and by so doing, is a way to keep the calculations of the lunar months in line with the solar year.[48] The solar calendar, however, is not used for the determination of festival days and is essentially a civic rather than religious calendar. This is discussed below.

Plethon's festivals or holidays, *hieromenias*, are based on the lunar cycle. These are *noumenia*, sacred to Zeus, on the first of the month, an unnamed day on the 8th, *dichomenia* on the 15th, an unnamed day on the 22nd, *hene*, sacred to Hades, on the 29th day of a full month, and *hene kai nea*, a time for self-reflection and scrutiny, on the last day of the month. Hollow months of 29 days lack the *hene* celebration. The first month of the year has an additional two celebrations on the 2nd and 3rd day of the month, following *noumenia*. The last month of the year has celebrations on the 27th and 28th days, preceding *hene kai nea*.[49]

Prayer, Again

Plethon's system of prayer, which he develops for groups rather than individuals, is relatively straightforward. Each day is divided into three parts, morning, noontime, and evening. Exactly how the day is divided into three is unknown. These may be likened to the prayer times found in Judaism and Islam, or the divine offices found in some forms of Christianity; however they are not quite the same as these. Prayer occurs during each of these times, though it is uncertain as to whether Plethon designated specific times for prayer or not. At whatever time prayer is to occur, the group gathers together and is led by a *hierokerux* or 'sacred herald,' a priest or priestess, someone chosen by the priest or priestess, or by a member of the group who is of good repute.

Each prayer session is devoted to a different deity or group of deities, though as we see in the works of pseudo-Dionysius, this can be easily expanded to angels and even saints. There are five

---

[47] C.f. Efthymios Nicolaidis. *Science and Eastern Orthodoxy. Johns Hopkins University Press, 2011, p. 121.*
[48] Temperance, "Solstices," http://baringtheaegis.blogspot.com/2013/08/solstices-and-calculations-on-hellenic.html.
[49] Anastos, "Calendar,"190, 237.

daily prayers: one in the morning, three in the afternoon, and one in the evening. Hymns are also sung during the afternoon sessions, with a hymn being sung between each of the noontime prayers. After this, a philosophical tract, or possibly a commentary, is read and expounded upon by the group's leader. Several of Plethon's hymns survive and have found their way into translation.[50]

There are also a number of movements related to how prayer is made, especially at the beginning of the prayer session. This adds a definite element of ritual and physicality to prayer. This is perhaps not surprising. In Platonism, a human is defined as a rational soul and body combined. By including both mind and body in prayer we are acting fully as humans. This also serves to enhance our understanding of humans as embodied things. A human is neither a soul nor a body, but both. In the Neoplatonism of Iamblichus, one of the main sources of inspiration for this Book of Hours, the goal is never to be entirely free of our body, but to act appropriately in relation to it and our soul's demiurgic activity.

The ritual motions of Plethon's prayers are not overly complex. The motions symbolically connect the supplicant with the sublunar and material gods, as well as the Demiurge. These movements make up a significant portion of the ritualization of prayer within this Book of Hours and are discussed in detail later.

A Theurgist's Calendar

Although Plethon is fully steeped in the traditions of Neoplatonism, his calendar is intended for general religious use. Anyone following his neo-pagan reform would be able to engage in regular worship by means of the calendar. That is true of our calendar as well. However, our calendar is also designed with the ritual theurgist in mind. As such, it contains a number of the patterns Plethon introduces, but is not limited to them. Our calendar has two major patterns: the movement of the moon, which dictates our ritual or liturgical month, and the pattern of the lunar months, each of which is associated with a different divinity or sacred persona.

---

[50] *Manuela Simeoni, translator, "Hymns to the Gods by George Gemistos Plethon," http://www.giornopaganomemoria.it/plethonhymns.html.*

The Movement of the Moon

Much of this has already been discussed above, and our calendar does not deviate greatly from Plethon's. However, there are blanks in Plethon's calendar as it has survived, in fragments, over the last several centuries. We know, generally, what the *hieromenias* of *noumenia*, *hene*, and *hene kai nea* were about. That leaves another three regular observations, *dichomenia*, and the two unnamed celebrations on the 8th of the month, what we call *deuteroebdomo*, the second seventh or the second group of seven days, and the 22nd, *phthinontos*, the fourth group of seven days, unaccounted. There are also the days immediately before and after the new moon that begins the year, the exact purpose of which has now been lost. These are discussed more fully below.

The Lunar Months

The twelve lunar months, and the thirteenth embolismic month, have been associated with a number of Olympic gods, and in different orders, over the last few thousand years. Herodotus includes the following in his Dodekatheon, or list of the twelve Olympic gods: Zeus, Hera, Poseidon, Hermes, Athena, Apollo, Alpheus, Cronus, Rhea, and the Charities. He also says that some include Hercules in this list. Others include Zeus, Hera, Poseidon, Demeter, Athena, Hestia, Apollo, Artemis, Ares, Aphrodite, Hephaestus, and Hermes. Yet others exclude Hestia and include Dionysus. These, however, are not related to particular months.

As stated previously, Plethon used the following order: Zeus, Poseidon, Hera, the Olympian gods, Apollo, Artemis, the gods of the sky, Athena, Dionysus, the Titans, Hephaestus, and the Daimons, with the thirteenth month being dedicated to all the gods. Plato also associated the twelve with the months, and may have associated Hades with the twelfth or thirteenth month. However, if there is a pattern here, its meaning has been lost. To find an order for our calendar, we will look to one of the most important Neoplatonists, Iamblichus of Chalcis.

Iamblichus is responsible for bringing theurgy fully into Neoplatonic practice. He also writes one, possibly two, treatises on the gods. Unfortunately, both have been lost. However, not all of his thoughts on the subject were lost with the texts. In a short treatise entitled *Concerning the Gods and the Universe*, Sallust, a philosopher under the employ of the Roman emperor Julian the Philosopher, and a student of a student of Iamblichus', writes about the twelve in a way similar to how Proclus, the 4th century head of the Athenian academy who was deeply influenced by the 'Divine Iamblichus', comes to view them.

In *Concerning the Gods*, the Dodekatheon are divided into four groups of three. The first group consists of Zeus, Poseidon, and Hephaestus, who create the world. The second group has Demeter, Hera, and Artemis, who animate it. Apollo, Aphrodite, and Hermes harmonize the world and Hestia, Athena, and Ares are its guardians. In Iamblichean theology, these are the leader gods and goddesses. Each soul has a leader god and is said to be in that deity's orbit, when viewed as one of the planetary gods, or, in Proclean terms, in that god's or goddess' series. From this, we can develop a system which moves through each of the groups, relating each lunar month to one of the gods, with their functions moving throughout the year:

God	Function	Month
Zeus-Helios	Creation	1
Demeter	Animation	2
Apollo	Harmonization	3
Hestia	Guardian	4
Poseidon	Creation	5
Hera	Animation	6
Aphrodite	Harmonization	7
Athena	Guardian	8
Hephaestus	Creation	9
Artemis	Animation	10
Hermes	Harmonization	11
Ares	Guardian	12

Why is Zeus transformed into Zeus-Helios? This has to do with Julian the Philosopher and his Iamblichean solar theology. According to Julian's *Hymn to King Helios*, Helios and Zeus are identical. This is important, because Helios is the celestial Demiurge, the ruler of the visible gods and leader of the leader gods, who are enumerated above. As our calendar is related to material theurgy and therefore to the visible gods and leader gods, and as the year begins with the Winter solstice, a festival especially related to Helios, it makes sense to represent that theology here.

The above list does leave us with the problem of the thirteenth month. For this we will turn to Plato, who possibly honours Hades at this time. This is similar to Plethon dedicating *hene*, at the end of the month, to Hades. Hades' function here would be that of completion and possibly rebirth, as Plato connects his final month not only to Hades but also to the spirits of the dead. This is associated with the Skira festival, held around June, and is related to the story of Persephone and Hades[51] and all that it implies, especially given late Platonism's belief in reincarnation.

The above only demonstrates the first of the major monthly cycles. The second cycle is derived from Proclean theology, and consists of 'seasons' of remaining, procession, and reversion from and to one's divine source. This overlaps the cycle of creation, animation, harmonization, and guarding as seen below:

---

[51] Gilman, "Twelve Gods and Seven Planets," http://cura.free.fr/decem/10kengil.html.

God	Activity	Movement	Month
Zeus-Helios	Creation	Remaining	1
Demeter	Animation		2
Apollo	Harmonization		3
Hestia	Guardian		4
Poseidon	Creation	Procession	5
Hera	Animation		6
Aphrodite	Harmonization		7
Athena	Guardian		8
Hephaestus	Creation	Reversion	9
Artemis	Animation		10
Hermes	Harmonization		11
Ares	Guardian		12

Although months may have been associated with a particular deity, they were not necessarily named that way. For instance, Plato's 13th month is named Skirophorion, after the Skira festival. Another month is called Hecatmmbaion, which refers to the 100 oxen sacrificed at this time. The month Metageitnion is named after a cult title of Apollo. That is, the names of the months are related to meaningful events or personae associated with that time.

As per Iamblichus, our calendar engages in the *interpretatio Graeca*. This way of understanding the gods of various polytheistic peoples sees different gods as cultural variations of the same set of basic deities. Iamblichus, in *De Mysteriis*, writes as an Egyptian priest, and makes many comparisons between Greek and Egyptian deities using this hermeneutic. As such, using the names of specific deities for the months is not only ahistorical, which is not necessarily a main concern for us, but also too limiting. Instead, it is more useful for us to employ names or titles that represent each divinity, and their variations, more broadly. While the following names are in Greek, in homage to the Hellenic origins of Neoplatonism, I believe they are also broad enough in meaning to encompass more than just the Greek gods from whom they are derived. However, not any title will do. Our calendar is not just a list of months, but representative of an overall cycle. As such, the names or titles of months must reflect the overall progression of the year and the month's role within it.

In this, the Greek correspondences are important. Sallust does not just enumerate the encosmic gods in relation to the four functions of creating, animating, harmonizing, and guarding. He also associates them with the seven planets, the four elements, and the ether or vault of the heavens. This is important for our next discussion, but also adds to the overall character of the realities with which we are dealing. In this scheme, Jupiter is attributed to Zeus(-Helios), Saturn to Demeter, the Sun to Apollo, the element of earth to Hestia, water to Poseidon, air to Hera, Venus to Aphrodite, the vault of the heavens to Athena, fire to Hephaestus, the moon to Artemis, Mercury to Hermes, and Mars to Ares. As we will see, this means there are sometimes two deities, two divine realities, associated with some of the planets. For now, we will see how these influence the overall themes of the lunar months.

Month	Title of the Month	Function	Movement	Greek Deity
1	Phyxiosion (Φυξιοσιών)	Creation	Mone (Remaining)	Zeus-Helios
2	Hôrêphorosion (Ωρηφοροσιών)	Animation		Demeter
3	Ouliosion (Ουλιοσιών)	Harmonization		Apollo
4	Escharaion (Ἐσχάραιών)	Guardian		Hestia
5	Ennosigaiosion (Εννοσιγαιοσιών)	Creation	Prohodos (Procession)	Poseidon
6	Antheiaion (Ανθειαιών)	Animation		Hera
7	Philomeidêsion (Φιλομειδησιών)	Harmonization		Aphrodite
8	Sôteiraion (Σωτειραιών)	Guardian		Athena
9	Polyphrônion (Πολυφριων)	Creation	Epistrophe (Return)	Hephaestus
10	Agrotereion (Αγροτερηιών)	Animation		Artemis
11	Diaktorosion (Διακτοροσιών)	Harmonization		Hermes
12	Khrysopêlêxion (Χρυσοπελεξιών)	Guardian		Ares
13	Nekrodegmônion (Νεκροδεγμωνιών)	Unification	Henosi (Union)	Hades

The liturgical theme of the first four months, from approximately mid-December to mid-March, reflect the term of Mone, abiding or remaining the soul does with its source. This is both the ending and starting point of the soul's eternal circular movement. This cycle continues even when, rarely, *henosis*, or divine union, begins. This is due to the dual-nature of the human soul: it inclines simultaneously both towards the eternal and the temporal. In order to be fully itself, it must engage in both.

The first month of the liturgical year is titled Phyxiosion, Φυξιοσιών, meaning 'Puts to Flight,' or 'Banishes.' In the first creative month of the Remaining cycle, the idea of sovereignty is paramount. Although associated with the creative process, Phyxiosion does not deal with creation itself, but, in relation to Mone, that which is necessary to do before creation itself begins. This is key to the month's name. This is the ordering or subduing of the primaeval chaos so that order may reign. This process is found in myths such as Zeus' defeat of the Titans, the battles between the Tuatha de Danann and the Fomoire, the conflict between the Æsir and Jotunn, and the defeat of Tiamat by Marduk. It is also encapsulated in the beginning of Genesis, with the watery void representing the primaeval disorder.

The title Phyxiosion reflects the initial creative impulse, which puts to flight the chaos of the pre-created forces of proto-nature. Such forces are embodied by, or are wielded by, entities and groups of entities such as the Titans, Apep, Tiamat, the Formoire, and the Jottun, and similar entities and groups of entities. There is no movement here. The activities of the gods are the same as their conception of those activities. The gods abide, and in doing so, give a place for souls to remain as well. Divinities represented by this month include Zeus, El, Amon, Marduk, Thor, Jupiter, the Daghdha, Abraham, the tribe of Zebulon, the apostle Matthew, and the angel Gabriel.

Hôrêphorosion, Ὡρηφοροσιών, meaning 'Bringer of the Seasons,' is our second month. Here the activity of Remaining comes through the power of animation or life-giving. This comes from the noeric force through the life-giving divinity. As such, we see something of a switching of gears from the heavenly realm to the earthly, even if in its divine state. This pattern continues through the season of Mone, though it does not extend to the other seasons.

This represents the power of movement, which is not movement itself, but the ability to move, whether or not it is expressed. It is this movement that both necessitates the activity of procession and allows for the eventual reversion to our source. Without this noeric, animating power, there is no possibility of movement, only of remaining. This is well seen in the story of the abduction of Persephone. In this, Persephone's mother, Demeter, withdraws her support from the Earth, moving the seasons to an eternal winter. Demeter's power to move, either towards creation or away, is also the power to bring the seasons. Divinities represented by this month include Demeter, Ceres, Isis, the tribe of Ephraim, James the younger, and the angel Barchiel.

The third month of the Remaining cycle is Ouliosion, Ουλιοσιών, meaning 'the Sound of Health.' In Hellenic thought since Galen, health was associated with the harmony of the four humours, an idea that lasted well into modernity. The harmony of Remaining originates above the sublunar elements, but is also, ultimately, embodied within those elements and through understanding the lower we may gain an understanding of the higher. The idea of sound also implies harmony, especially when understood from a Pythagorean perspective and the Platonic idea that the gods are all perfect, and therefore perfectly harmonious. Here the animated soul is in harmony with its leader god, but is also in harmony with itself. As the soul is dual-natured, this harmony also means the eventual coming of Procession away from the source. It is no accident that the powers of the sun are related to this time. The sun, and its various divinities, are representative of the celestial Demiurgos. Understanding the harmonizing nature of this divinity allows us to also recognize the harmonizing nature of our own demiurgy. Divinities represented by this month include Helios, Apollo, Horus, Re, Jacob, the apostle Mathias, the angel Malchidiel, and the tribe of Dan.

The final month of the Remaining cycle is Escharaion, Ἐσχἀραιών, which essentially means 'Hearth.' Originally referring to a domestic hearth, or *hestia*, the word *eschara* eventually comes to refer to the top part of an altar of burnt sacrifice, where the burning coals are kept.[52] The hearth is a symbol of the security of the home. Neoplatonic thought does not subscribe to the common idea of needing to sacrifice to the gods in order to get some reward, or prevent some disaster. It does, however, see sacrifice as a foundational religious act, one that ultimately makes us more like, and brings us closer to, the divine. In this, the obvious fire symbolism of the hearth is superseded by its earthy nature. The hearth represents the home and the foundation of the home and family.

---

[52] Pieraccini, *Around the Hearth*, 163.

Divinities represented by this month include Hestia, Vesta, the apostle Thadeus, the angel Asmodel, and the tribe of Ruben.

The second cycle, Prohodos, Procession, begins with Ennosigaision, Εννοσιγαιοσιών, 'Shaker of the Earth,' which refers to Poseidon's role as the maker of earthquakes. While that may seem destructive rather than creative, earthquakes are also responsible for new landmasses being thrust out of the sea. This shaking is the beginning of the procession of the soul away from its source and ultimately down the river of the Milky Way. This changes everything for the soul, especially in its initial 'fall' from the heavens, as depicted in Plato's *Phaedrus* myth. The soul is not, of course, created here. Instead we may see the creative impulse of Ennosigaision's presiding divinity in the form of a new kind of movement, one which ultimately leads to the soul's perfection. Divinities represented by this month include Poseidon, Neptune, Nodens, Manannán MacLir, Manawydan fab Llyr, Ægir, Simon, Ambriel, and the tribe of Judah.

The month corresponding to the activity of Animation of Procession is Antheiaion, Ανθειαιών, meaning 'Blooming,' 'Friend of Flowers,' or 'Of the Flowers.' Where Ennosigaision celebrates the impulse towards Procession, Antheiaion celebrates the movement of Procession itself. Divinities represented by this month include Hera, Juno, Isis, John, Muriel, and the tribe of Judah.

The third month of the Procession cycle, Philomeidêsion, Φιλομειδησιών, is the month of Harmonization. The name of this month is 'Laughter-Loving,' which is similar to titles associated with the goddess Hathor, such as 'Mistress of the House of Jubilation' and 'The One Who Fills the Sanctuary with Joy.' The procession of the soul, whether leading directly into incarnation or not, is not, of itself, a bad thing. Instead, it is a thing of Necessity, deemed as such by the all-good celestial Demiurge. This month represents the soul's understanding of this necessity, and its eventual harmonization with it, transforming Fate into Providence, and with this comes the joy of sacred laughter. Divinities represented by this month include Aphrodite, Venus, Hathor, Frig, Freya, Peter, Verchiel, and the tribe of Asher.

Sôteiraion, Σωτειραιών, is the final month of the Procession cycle, corresponding to the activity of Guarding. Its name means 'saviour.' While saviour may have a physical connotation, it is also applied to spiritual salvation. This is certainly seen with Christ, but also with Helios and Zeus, both of whom have this title. The placement of Athena here is important, as Sallust places the pneuma above the spheres of the planets. This pneuma is the source of the pneumatic vehicle of the soul, and it is this vehicle that takes us to the realm of generation and ultimately, when purified, returns us safely home. Divinities represented by this month include Athena, Minerva, Sophia, Neith, Sulis, Andrew, Hamaliel, and the tribe of Simeon.

Polyphrônion, Πολυφρωνιών, the first month of the season of Epistrophê, Return, variously means 'Very Wise,' 'Ingenious,' and 'Inventive.' This refers to proficiency at many different crafts and is arguably a demiurgic title. The soul beginning the return to its source has become exactly this, a demiurge, willingly engaging with the work of divine creation. The creative work generally associated with the divinities of this month is sublunar in nature. While the purified soul functions both in and above the realm of generation and the moon, it must descend fully into physical incarnation before its ascent is possible. Divinities represented by this month include Hephaestus, Vulcan, Ptah, Wayland, Goibniu, Gofannon, Gobannos, Bartholemew, Zuriel, and the tribe of Issachar.

The second, Animating month of Return is Agroterêion, Αγροτερηιών, the month of 'the Hunt' or the 'Huntress.' The hunt is a thing of movement and life, but one that relies upon death; the soul does not return home while still incarnate. In this, the moonlit hunt is also symbolic of the return to our source, a return that takes us beyond the sphere of the moon, to the divine realm above. Divinities represented by this month include Artemis, Diana, Isis, Arduinna, Arianrhod, Skadi, Philip, Barbiel, and the tribe of Benjamin.

Diaktorosion, Διακτοροσιών means 'Messenger,' 'Minister,' and 'Guide,' and is the third, Harmonizing month of Return. The month's name alludes to the role of the guide and messenger who brings word from the divine; be it a philosopher, hero, daimon or our leader god. This is a harmonizing act, as it brings the world, and the supplicant, in harmony with divine providence. The kinds of divinities associated with this month are psychopomps, leading the purified soul back home. Divinities represented by this month include Hermes, Mercurius, Djehuti, Anpu, Odin, Lugh, James the Elder, Adnachiel, and the tribe of Naphtali.

The Guardian month of Return is Khrysopêlêxion, Χρυσοπελεξσιών, meaning 'of the Golden Helm.' The golden helm is a relic of the sun, represented by the aureole. Although this month is not representative of the sun, it does immediately proceed Phyxios, and can be seen as employing the coming of the solar light to protect the soul, not only in its ascent home, but in its inevitable descent towards generation. This light also protects and guides the theurgist as they return to their leader god, and ultimately to the celestial demiurgos, represented by the sun itself. Divinities represented by this month include Ares, Mars, Neith, Nodens, Tyr, Nuada, Isaac, Thomas, Hanael, and the tribe of Gad.

The embolismic month is Nekrodegmônion, Νεκροδεγμωνιών, 'Receiver of the Dead.' Standing outside of both lunar monthly cycles, this month can be said to represent the underworld and the sub-lunar gods. However, ritual death is also a common part of initiation, including the influential Chaldean ritual of ascension to the celestial Demiurgos. One must descend before one can rise up again. Through this process *henosis*, union with the divine, occurs. Divinities represented by this month include Hades, Plouton, Midir, Hekate as Queen of Daimons, Hel, Mary Magdalene or Judas, and Joseph.

CHAPTER 3

Hieromenias and the Prayer Service

This chapter focuses on the themes of the holidays. There are two kinds of celebrations found in any given month. One is related to the yearly or 'seasonal' cycle, the other to the lunar cycle.

Yearly Hieromenias

The lunar vigils and feasts are only part of the calendar. Although they cycle throughout the year, they are subordinate to two other cycles. The first of these has already been discussed and is connected to the divine powers ruling over each month. Although Plethon's calendar does not use this system exactly, ours is ultimately based on his. The second cycle is modelled on Proclus' theory of the movement of the soul: Remaining Proceeding, and Reverting. Unlike the other cycle, this is unique to our calendar and is a series of seasons related to the movement of the soul. This is not necessarily related to the movement of the soul in a single incarnation, but through many incarnations as the soul becomes perfected. Each of the yearly hieromenia seasons start at the beginning of each of the months associated with the cycle of creation. The beginning of each season is marked by hieromenia of the same name. Together, these two cycles modify the lunar observances.

Mone (Μονή): Remaining

The liturgical season of Mone, Remaining, begins with Phyxiosion, the month associated with Zeus-Helios and creation, the beginning of the liturgical calendar. The festival of Mone lasts from the two days before Hene kai Nea to the second day after Noumenia on the last and first months of the year. Mone is a New Year's celebration, but also marks a time of 'internal' spiritual work.

This season represents the phase of the soul when it abides with the One and its leader gods and guardian or guiding divinities. As such, the theurgic work of this season should reflect this remaining, and the *hieromenia* itself is connected to the pre-essential Demiurgos.[53] This beginning of this season, as the New Year, is celebrated from two days before the first of Phyxiosion through two days afterwards.

Prohodos (Πρόοδος): Procession

The season of Prohodos, Procession, begins with the fifth lunar month, Ennosigaiosion, connected to Poseidon. The formal celebration of the beginning of this season lasts from the day before to the day after the first day of Ennosigaision. Procession is the phase of the soul when it is away from its source in what might be considered its most 'active' period. This is when the soul works to remember its source and true nature. For those that have already accomplished this, Prohodos is the time when the soul is most actively engaged in demiurgy and the governance of the generative realm, and is so appropriately connected to the celestial Demiurgos.

Epistrophe (Επιστροφή): Reversion

The normally final season of Reversion begins with the ninth month of Polyphrônion. The beginning of this season is celebrated the day before, on, and the day after the beginning of Polyphrônion, the month of Hephaestus. In all cases, the primary day of celebration, or observation, is on Noumenia, the midnight after the new moon which begins the lunar month. Reversion is the phase of the soul which corresponds to returning from whence it came: its leader god and, ultimately, the One. For the purified soul, this is the natural recognition that it has completed the work necessary to it and it is now time to return home for rejuvenation. For the rest of us it may be the interval between incarnations which are forced upon us due to our spiritual impurity. In either case, it is the journey back to where we started. Also in either case we will abide for a time, and then proceed once more. The season of Epistrophe is connected to the sublunar

---

53 *More information about the various Demiurgoi, as well as the greater kinds or divine hierarchy in general, can be found in* Living Theurgy.

Demiurgos who often manifests as a god of the underworld. This is because before we can return, we must end this cycle of incarnation. This can mean literal death, or the ritualized death and ascension ceremonies of initiation.

Henosi (Ἕνωση): Union

The season of Union is somewhat apart from the other three. First, it only occurs when there is an intercalated month. Second, it is only a month long, calling for a more intense approach to the work of the season. Third, it is not part of Proclus' theory, although he does speak of *henosis* or union with the gods and/or the One. The season of Henosi contains many of the themes of Mone and Noumenia. However, Mone does not necessarily imply union with our sources, it can just as well be the time when we are once again following the circuit of our leader through the heavenly realm. The season brings about a time of intense concentration on our leader, and associated series, if known, or discovering them if not. As such, it is also a time of concentration on the personal daimon, who leads us in our circuit with the divine. Henosi is celebrated from the day before through the day after the beginning of Nekrodegmônion. The season is connected to the Agathos Daimon, the 'good spirit' who is often seen as a manifestation of pre-essential and celestial Demiurgoi, the guardian daimon of one's family, and the personal daimon.

Lunar Hieromenia

This Book of Hours celebrates six recurring, monthly, lunar holidays, three annually recurring holidays connected to the cycle of remaining, proceeding, and reverting, and sacred days at the beginning of Nekrodegmônion. During any given month, there may be from five to eight observances, covering one or more days.

There are five observances common to every month, and a sixth common to all full months of 30 lunar days. These observances, vigils, or *hieromenias*, flow through the movement of the lunar month in accordance with the lunar phases. The exception to this is Hene, which only occurs on the day before Hene kai Nea, the day of the new moon, during a full month.

Noumenia (Νουμηνια): New Moon

Noumenia is the first day of each lunar month, occurring the day after the dark of the moon. In Plethon's calendar, this day is sacred to Zeus. In this, Plethon follows a long tradition stretching from Plutarch and Hesiod to Porphyry and Proclus, who place the tradition at Plato's feet.[54] Given the connection Iamblichus' school of Neoplatonism, especially as espoused by Julian the Philosopher, makes between Zeus and Helios, Noumenia is sacred to the celestial Demiurgos, the all-good creator god of the *Timaeus*. As the first day of the month, honouring the Demiurgos is fitting. Just as the Demiurgos is the leader of the leader gods, Noumenia is the leader of its month.

Deuteroebdomo (Δεύτεροέβδομο): Second Seventh

None of Plethon's writings on the three feasts of Deuteroebdomo, Dichomenia, and Phthinontos have survived. As such, we have to interpolate, as far as possible, what these median days of the month might mean. Following the above plan, Deuteroebdomo, the 8th day of the month, or beginning of the second week, celebrates the daimons. Iamblichus tells of us three different kinds of daimon, the first of which is the personal daimon, the *oikeios daimon*, which is dealt with during Hene kai Nea. The other two are 'evil' daimons, and those who oversee the physical world. The evil daimons are described as those who punish evil-doers, as well as guardian daimons; those which protect either places or families. These daimons can advise us on proper moral activity and can help those who are in the moral right. The other kind of daimon is described in terms similar to the modern idea of an elemental; a simple being with a particular, genegogic function. Both these kinds of daimons are honoured at this time of the lunar cycle.

Dichomenia (Διχομηνια): Split Moon

The beginning of the third week, the 15th day of the lunar month, and the full moon, moves from daimons to heroes. In Greek mythology, heroes are typically semi-divine beings, demigods, given to magnificent feats. In other religions they might be seen as the founders of religion, such

---

[54] Anastos, "Calendar," 238.

as the Jewish patriarchs and matriarchs,[55] or legendary people such as the Irish Fionn mac Cumhaill and his son Oisín. They are figures who are greater than life, and exemplars of living virtuous lives, being capable of things even the most purified human souls are not. The role of heroes is to spur us on to lead virtuous lives. The prayers for Dichomenia revolve around heroes in general.

Traditionally, the new moon, and the days leading up to it, beginning with Noumenia, are considered a time of prosperity, with Dichomenia being the height of this time. After this day, leading to Hene kai Nea, the days are considered to represent decrease rather than increase.[56] As we'll see below, this can also be connected to the idea of turning inwards, as opposed to the outward-facing elements of the previous holy days.

Phthinontos (Φθίνοντος): Descending [Moon]

The 22nd of the month, the beginning of the fourth week, moves to the least of the divine beings: purified souls. This day marks a celebration of the ancestors, including our own. However, it also includes the honouring of purified human souls, those great figures who incarnate purposefully and without identifying themselves with their bodies. These are the saints, prophets, theurgists, and other great figures such as Pythagoras and Socrates, found in numerous religious traditions. These are those souls which represent the pinnacle of humanity, whose philosophy and theurgy help illuminate the world.

Hene (Ἕνε): Old [Moon]

The day before Hene kai Nea during full months is, according to Plethon's calendar, sacred to Pluton. Pluton is described as a form of, or one of, the sub-lunar Demiurge. Iamblichus intimates that Pluton is the god who rules over all the personal daimons, presumably in addition to their leader gods. Connected to the god of the underworld, Hene is an appropriate time for the contemplation of death and acts as a bridge between the celebration of the ancestors a few days

---

55 *It is arguable, however, that these are more representatives of purified souls than heroes.*
56 *Anastos, 'Calendar,' 244-5.*

before, and reflection on our own life and death and personal daimon the next day. Although it may seem morbid to contemplate death, it must be remembered that the purpose, or at least a purpose, of philosophy is to prepare us for death, about which we should have no fear but which we should instead embrace when our time comes.[57]

Hene kai Nea (Ἕνε καὶ Νέα): Old and the New [Moons]

Plethon tells us the last day of the month is a time for self-reflection and scrutiny. To this we may connect the Delphic Maxim:

> *Take careful council,*
> *Know thyself,*
> *Consult the daimon,*
> *Undertake nothing without God.*[58]

To take careful council and to know ourselves requires reflection, but connected to this is the consultation of the daimon and acting only with God. This final injunction is met throughout the rest of the month, so it is the personal daimon, as part of our self-reflection, which Hene kai Nea focuses upon instead. This does not look at personal daimons in general, however, but *our* personal daimon. As such, Hene kai Nea is an intensely personal time, and more a vigil than a feast or celebration in the common sense of the word.

Plethon's Prayer Service

A Theurgist's Book of Hours is written both with groups and the individual in mind. As there are no significant differences between the structures of group or solo practice, I focus on the group version below. This has historical precedence in Plethon, and I provide notes later concerning how it might be modified for the individual. Also, the following, as being derived from the original pagan format, retains pagan language. Again, I later discuss how modifications to the language might be made for non-Greek-focused pagans and monotheists.

---

[57] *Phaedo 61c-69e.*
[58] *Betz, "Delphic," 159-60.*

The following is derived from what remains of Plethon's liturgy.[59] Plethon divided the day into three parts: 1) morning before breakfast, or before the work day, 2) the afternoon, any time before dinner, and 3) evening, after dinner and before bed. Although Plethon does not exactly use this terminology, these can be referred to as *Eothinos*, Dew; *Mesembria*, Noontide; and *Esperinos*, Evensong.[60] On non-hieromenia days, five prayers, literally *prosreseis*[61] or 'praise,' are recited over the three prayer periods. One is recited at Dew, three at Noontide, and one at Evensong. Hymns are sung between each prayer during the Noontide service, and a call to prayer is announced before each service. In general, worship of the divine hierarchies should be performed in temples or shrines, or in a place free of the *miasma*, spiritual contagion, from sources such as human bones and excrement.[62]

Worship is to be led or supervised by a *hierokerux* or 'sacred herald,' a priest or someone chosen by a priest, or the most respected layperson present.[63] This person makes the call to prayer:

> *Worshippers of the gods give ear.*
> *This is the hour for the dew (or the noontide, or the evensong) prayer to the gods.*
> *Let us invoke all the gods and Zeus,*
> *who reigns over them, with all our mind,*
> *and all our reason, and all our soul.*[64]

This call is made once on non-hieromenia days, twice on all hieromenia except Noumenia, and three times on Noumenia, including those which begin one of the seasons. Immediately after the call, everyone kneels on both knees, looks upward and raises their arms with their hands palm up in a welcoming gesture and says "O gods, be propitious." This is repeated twice more, the first time with a knee raised and the right hand touching the ground, then with the left hand touching the ground. The first call is general, the second calls upon the Olympic or celestial gods, and the third the rest of the gods, or possibly the sub-lunar gods. Finally, both knees and hands are placed

---

[59] See both Anastos, "Calendar," 1948 and Gandz, "Calendar-Reform," 1950. Unless otherwise noted, all information concerning Plethon's prayer service is derived from these sources. See also Kupperman, Living Theurgy, 168-9.
[60] C.f. Anastos, "Calendar," 252.
[61] Ibid.
[62] Ibid., 255.
[63] Ibid.
[64] Ibid.

on the ground, and, with the head touching the ground, all say "O Zeus, the King, be propitious" three times.

Plethon even tells us which musical modes are to be used. The first call, with both hands in the air, is to be in the Hypophrygian mode, the second, to the celestial gods, in the Phrygian, and the final in the Hypodorian mode. That forms of the Dorian and Phyrigian modes are used, and no others, is not surprising. In the *Republic*, Plato rejects all the modes except these as being inappropriate to the perfect city. Of what remains, the Dorian mode is stern and solemn, reminding us of what "a brave man utters in warlike action and in stern resolve; and when his cause is failing, and he is going to wounds or death or is overtaken by disaster in some other form, at every such crisis he meets the blows of fortune with firm step and a determination to endure." Of the Phrygian mode, we are told it is the "opposite kind [from the Dorian mode] for times of peace and freedom of action, when there is no pressure of necessity, and he is seeking to persuade God by prayer, or man by instruction and admonition, or when on the other hand he is expressing his willingness to yield to the persuasion or entreaty or admonition of others. And when in this manner he has attained his end, I would have the music show him not carried away by his success, but acting moderately and wisely in all circumstances, and acquiescing in the event."[65]

The hymns are also to be accompanied by music. As with the opening invocations, the musical modes Plethon discusses are those found in Plato, expanded to include both forms of the Phrygian and Dorian modes: Hypophrygian, Phrygian, Hypodorian and Dorian. Although evidence suggests Plethon modelled this after Byzantine Christian prayer services,[66] it is difficult to tell if his hymns use the classical Greek form of the modes, or the altered forms current to his own times. In either case, different hymns are assigned different modes, and these are related to different days of the liturgical week, suggesting different days have appropriately different moods in terms of worship.

There is also symbolism in the four gestures of invocation. The second gesture, kneeling on one knee and touching the ground with the right hand, is the gesture of "worshipp[ing] the gods

---

[65] *Rep* III.398E-399C.
[66] Anastos, "Calendar," 268.

of Olympus."[67] In an Iamblichean context, these are the leader, visible or encosmic gods; the celestial gods of the seven ancient planets, the elements, and the fiery ether[68]: Kronos, Zeus, Ares, Apollo, Aphrodite, Hermes, Selene, Athena, Hephaistos, Hera, Poseidon, and Hestia. These are the twelve divine powers to which our liturgical months are dedicated. The third gesture, of kneeling on one knee and touching the ground with the left hand, is connected to the "worship of the rest of the gods,"[69] possibly chthonic or sublunar divinities, including Pluton or Hades, but also daimons,[70] to which I would add heroes and purified souls. The first gesture, kneeling on both knees, hands raised into the air, is left unexplained, but from the above context can be seen as a supplication to the liminal or invisible gods that exist above the leader gods.

The origin of these gestures, and the words associated with them, is somewhat questionable. While there is evidence of these in pagan literature and ancient statues, they also reflect Byzantine modes of worship, and Plethon is deeply entrenched in both of these. He even quotes the Bible. So it seems likely he is drawing from multiple sources, both pagan and Christian.[71]

After this opening, the prayer leader announces the prayer to be recited while all rest upon both knees. Finally, someone selected beforehand recites the prayer of the hour. In the case of the hymns between prayers during Noontide, all present sing or chant them. After the formal prayers, the hierokerux, priest, or chosen person then reads from, or expounds upon, a philosophical or sacred text. This may have been Plato, Pythagoras, or possibly even Zoroaster, or a commentary from Proclus or Iamblichus.

A Theurgic Modification – Dammit, Jim, I'm a Theurgist, not a Layman!

Even though Plethon forms the basis of this work, there is at least one significant difference between his reform and this: Plethon's work is intended to be for the average religious practitioner, or at least one is who is not explicitly a theurgist, and for devotion to the Greek

---

[67] *Ibid.,*   255.
[68] *Elsewhere, I have associataed these with the Dionysian angelic choir of Thrones. See Living Theurgy, 122-128.*
[69] *Ibid.*
[70] *Ibid., 259.*
[71] *Ibid., 257-60.*

pantheon. Such a practitioner may know relatively little, or even nothing, of the Neoplatonic underpinnings of Plethon's service, and that wouldn't really matter. While *this* text could be utilized in such a way, it is also intended for Neoplatonists and theurgists, and not necessarily those dedicated to the deities of Hellas. As such, some changes are in order. First, there is a slight modification to the initial call to prayer and supplication of the gods. The divinities worshipped by prayers and hymns are titular in nature, rather than using specific proper names. There is also a change to the final part of the prayer session: the reading of sacred or philosophical texts and/or commentaries on those texts to a *lectio divina* practice.

In Plethon, the readings were held during the extended noontide prayer session. Today, this may prove impossible given work schedules and modern life; an evening or morning reading may make more sense for many people. Instead of specifying when to engage in the readings, suggested readings will be included at the end of each prayer section. For the seasonal hieromenia only a few suggestions will be made. For those which are repeated throughout the year I make several suggestions.

It is unclear what Plethon intends by the reading of these texts, whether or not they were to be passively received or actively participated in. As participants may not have had any philosophical backgrounds, it is plausible this was meant to be passive rather than active performance. For a Neoplatonic audience, however, this is not necessarily enough, especially as such readings can have a theurgic function, which, as we've seen in Iamblichus, requires purposeful, intellectual, activity, rather than passive receptivity.[72] As such, it seems appropriate to transform the reading into an activity. In *Living Theurgy* I present a Neoplatonic variation of the Christian practice of *lectio divina*. Perhaps significantly, the foundations of this Christian practice come from the 3rd century theologian Origen, a Christian Neoplatonist. This somewhat modified form of the practice follows.

Begin by quieting, so far as possible, the chattering of the mind and settling into an inner silence. When everyone is ready, or in the case of an individual practice, when you are ready, read aloud a passage deemed appropriate to the time. This can be from a sacred text, a philosophical text, or a commentary on either. Several examples are given in the Praxis section below, but you

---

[72] C.f. DM II.11, 115.

are not limited to those passages. If possible, keep the passage short so it may be more readily retained. This is especially important for groups where only one person has a copy of the text. Read the text slowly and clearly. The main activity here is listening: understand, but do not respond.

After reading comes contemplation. If working by yourself, it may be possible to memorize the text to allow each word to sink more deeply into your mind, though memorization is not required. Let each word weigh heavily in your mind, but do not look for specific meanings. This is not a dialectical practice. If you find yourself distracted, simply turn your attention back to the passage. Take as much time as you feel, or the group feels, necessary for this. Never rush any part of this, or any, contemplative practice.

When you feel you have gained all you can from this step, it is time to respond. Although contemplation relies upon intuitive knowing, this is the time for dialectic and discursive reasoning based on the insight gained through contemplation, which is something of a reversal of the dialectic process. What do you or the gathering think the passage means? Why? Is your reasoning sound? This is a time of critical thinking, but not a time for criticism. If members of the group have different opinions, they should be presented in an unthreatening way. Everyone gathered is there for the same reason and there is no reason for aggression. All present should review their thought processes and talk out their reasonings. Finding holes in argumentation is to everyone's advantage, and is Socrates' very process in the Dialogues. If a line of reasoning cannot be supported, or the support crumbles, remove it, and repeat this until there is nothing left except what can be rationally supported.

Take some time between this and the next step for everyone to clear their minds. When ready, respond once again to the reading. Or, rather, respond to your responses, combining the experiences of the internal contemplation and the external dialectic. Righting the uplifting discursive process, this is an opportunity to participate the divine Intellect and speak not from the discursive mind but from intuitive knowing: gnosis. For this portion, even with a group, this may be spoken aloud or the in stillness of the mind.

The last step is to let everything go; the thoughts, the contemplations, the words and ideas resulting from these. Words are no longer necessary as the contemplation, for that is what *lectio divina* is, moves from an active, external process to an internal, apophatic process, where what was gained is taken away. Everyone may allow themselves to connect to that part of reality, so far as possible, that is beyond sound and action.

Other Modifications – From the Many to the One

As already noted, Plethon's liturgy is intended for groups. Fortunately, approaching this as an individual requires very little modification. In terms of the call to worship, in theory, nothing needs to be changed. It may seem to make sense to drop the opening line: "Worshippers of the gods give ear." There is, after all, only one worshipper, the theurgist themselves, and they, as the speaker, is already listening. However, I suggest this passage can have a deeper meaning, as we might expect from a Platonically inspired form of worship. We may interpret this as a sign not simply to listen up, in a physical sense, but also in a spiritual sense. The worshipper of the gods, or of God, is not just the theurgist, but the soul, which seeks to know itself and once more find its place in its proper divine orbit. As such, this is a call for the soul to remember itself, its place in creation, and its divine series. The call is anagogic or uplifting. The very first sentence begins the theurgic process at the heart of the service, which is discussed below.

While the first sentence of the liturgical call to prayer is retained, even for individual practice, there are at least two changes which must logically be made. First, the prayers and hymns given below are in the plural. The individual will have to decide to either change these to the singular or retain the plural, using the above ideology: it is not only the theurgist praying, but their soul as well. Either are plausible readings as, while we are not our souls but our souls mixed with a physical body, our souls are still part of us. Second, in Plethon's liturgy, a hierokerux or other religious specialist oversees the service, and a number of people participate, through the reading or recitation of prayers, group hymns, or the contemplation of sacred texts. This isn't possible with an individual. The solo theurgist is responsible for the entire service.

This necessarily changes the pacing of the service. With a group, everyone's experience is important, and the hierokerux needs to make sure everyone has an opportunity to at some point participate, has enough time to contemplate a reading, and generally make sure everything is organized. It is also possible that everyone will want to recite prayers and hymns rather than have one person designated to do so. The individual theurgist needs to be only concerned with themself. This greatly increases the theurgist's need to self-monitor, as there is no one else to act as interlocutor. For the experienced practitioner, this will likely have already become an integrated practice, but for the beginner, this kind of self-awareness is not only of great importance but can also be difficult as they lose themselves in the moment.

Plethon, as should be clear, had a Greek audience in mind for his liturgy. Anastos persuasively argues throughout his paper that regardless of Plethon's sources, pagan or Christian, the ultimate source of his thought is Greek. However not all theurgists, or even Neoplatonists, have a Greek or Hellenic focus. As such, and as previously noted, this Book of Hours does not use proper names in the following hymns, but epitaphs, which often relate to multiple divinities. It should be entirely possible for individual practitioners, or groups, to make suitable changes, if desired, to reflect their particular worship and theurgic praxes.

Interlude: On Organization

The remainder of this book consists of liturgical calendars, prayers,[73] and hymns[74] appropriate to each sacred month, and is divided into four chapters. As in traditional books of hours, the first chapter of the praxis section, chapter four, contains full liturgical calendars from 2021-2026 and then lists the years with intercalary months through the end of the 21st century. The following chapters cover the yearly, lunar, and monthly *hieromenias*.

For convenience, the opening call to prayer and supplication to the gods is given with the first set of prayers in each of the following chapters, but not for every prayer service. Words to be spoken are in regular type, instructions and actions are *italicized*, and speakers are **bold**.

---

[73] *Prayers are written in free verse.*
[74] *Hymns are written in 8.7.8.7D meter.*

Kronos

PRAXIS

Part II: Praxis

CHAPTER 4

Liturgical Calendars

2021

Phyxiosion
Noumenia & Mone: 1/13
Mone:1/14
Deuteroebdomo: 1/20
Dichomenia: 1/28
Phthinontos: 2/4
Hene kai Nea: 2/12

Hôrêphorosion
Noumenia: 2/13
Deuteroebdomo: 2/19
Dichomenia: 2/27
Phthinontos: 3/5
Hene: 3/12
Hene kai Nea: 3/13

Ouliosion
Noumenia: 3/14
Deuteroebdomo: 3/21
Dichomenia: 3/28
Phthinontos: 4/4
Hene kai Nea: 4/11

Escharaion
Noumenia: 4/12
Deuteroebdomo: 4/20
Dichomenia: 4/26
Phthinontos: 5/3
Hene kai Nea & Prohodos: 5/11

Ennosigaiosion
Noumenia & Prohodos: 5/12
Prohodos: 5/13
Deuteroebdomo: 5/19
Dichomenia: 5/26
Phthinontos: 6/2
Hene: 6/9
Hene kai Nea: 6/10

Antheiaion
Noumenia: 6/11
Deuteroebdomo: 6/17
Dichomenia: 6/24
Phthinontos: 7/1
Hene kai Nea: 7/9

Philomeidêsion
Noumenia: 7/10
Deuteroebdomo: 7/17
Dichomenia: 7/23
Phthinontos: 7/31
Hene: 8/7
Hene kai Nea: 8/8

Sôteiraion
Noumenia: 8/9
Deuteroebdomo: 8/15
Dichomenia: 8/22
Phthinontos: 8/30
Hene kai Nea & Epistrophê: 9/6

Polyphrônion
Noumenia & Epistrophê: 9/7
Epistrophê: 9/8
Deuteroebdomo: 9/13
Dichomenia: 9/20
Phthinontos: 9/28
Hene: 10/5
Hene kai Nea: 10/6

Agroterêion
Noumenia: 10/7
Deuteroebdomo: 10/12
Dichomenia: 10/20
Phthinontos: 10/28
Hene kai Nea: 11/3

Diaktorosion
Noumenia: 11/4
Deuteroebdomo: 11/11
Dichomenia: 11/19
Phthinontos: 11/27
Hene: 12/3
Hene kai Nea: 12/4

Khrysopêlêxion
Noumenia: 12/5
Deuteroebdomo: 12/10
Dichomenia: 12/18
Fthinonto: 12/26
Mone: 1/1/22
Hene kai Nea & Mone: 1/2

2022

Phyxiosion
Noumenia & Mone: 1/3/22
Mone: 1/4-5
Deuteroebdomo: 1/9
Dichomenia: 1/17
Phthinontos: 1/25
Hene: 1/30
Hene kai Nea: 1/31

Hôrêphorosion
Noumenia: 2/1
Deuteroebdomo: 2/8
Dichomenia: 2/16
Phthinontos: 2/23
Hene kai Nea: 3/2

Ouliosion
Noumenia: 3/3
Deuteroebdomo: 3/10
Dichomenia: 3/18
Phthinontos: 3/25
Hene: 3/31
Hene kai Nea: 4/1

Escharaion
Noumenia: 4/2
Deuteroebdomo: 4/9
Dichomenia: 4/16
Phthinontos: 4/23
Hene kai Nea & Prohodos: 4/30

Ennosigaiosion
Noumenia & Prohodos: 5/1
Prohodos: 5/2
Deuteroebdomo: 5/8
Dichomenia: 5/16
Phthinontos: 5/22
Hene: 5/29
Hene kai Nea: 5/30

Antheiaion
Noumenia: 5/31
Deuteroebdomo: 6/7
Dichomenia: 6/14
Phthinontos: 6/20
Hene kai Nea: 6/28

Philomeidêsion
Noumenia: 6/29
Deuteroebdomo: 7/6
Dichomenia: 7/13
Phthinontos: 7/20
Hene kai Nea: 7/28

Sôteiraion
Noumenia: 7/29
Deuteroebdomo: 8/5
Dichomenia: 8/11
Phthinontos: 8/18
Hene: 8/26
Hene kai Nea & Epistrophê: 8/27

Polyphrônion
Noumenia & Epistrophê: 8/28
Epistrophê: 8/29
Deuteroebdomo: 9/3

Dichomenia: 9/10
Phthinontos: 9/17
Hene kai Nea: 9/25

Agroterêion
Noumenia: 9/26
Deuteroebdomo: 10/2
Dichomenia: 10/9
Phthinontos: 10/17
Hene: 10/24
Hene kai Nea: 10/25

Diaktorosion
Noumenia: 10/26
Deuteroebdomo: 11/1
Dichomenia: 11/8
Phthinontos: 11/16
Hene kai Nea: 11/23

Khrysopêlêxion
Noumenia: 11/24
Deuteroebdomo: 11/30
Dichomenia: 12/7
Fthinonto: 12/16
Hene: 12/22
Hene kai Nea & Henosis: 12/23

Nekrodegmônion
Noumenia & Henosis: 12/24
Henosis: 12/25
Deuteroebdomo: 12/29
Dichomenia: 1/6
Fthinonto: 1/14
Mone: 1/19
Hene kai Nea & Mone: 1/20

2023

Phyxiosion
Noumenia & Mone: 1/21
Mone: 1/22-23
Deuteroebdomo: 1/28
Dichomenia: 2/5
Phthinontos: 2/13
Hene kai Nea: 2/20

Hôrêphorosion
Noumenia: 2/21
Deuteroebdomo: 2/27
Dichomenia: 3/7
Phthinontos: 3/14
Hene kai Nea: 3/21

Ouliosion
Noumenia: 3/22
Deuteroebdomo: 3/28
Dichomenia: 4/5
Phthinontos: 4/13
Hene kai Nea: 4/19

Escharaion
Noumenia: 4/20
Deuteroebdomo: 4/27
Dichomenia: 5/5
Phthinontos: 5/12
Hene: 5/18
Hene kai Nea & Prohodos: 5/19

Ennosigaiosion
Noumenia & Prohodos: 5/20
Prohodos: 5/21
Deuteroebdomo: 5/27
Dichomenia: 6/6
Phthinontos: 6/10
Hene kai Nea: 6/17

Antheiaion
Noumenia: 6/18
Deuteroebdomo: 6/26
Dichomenia: 7/3
Phthinontos: 7/9
Hene kai Nea: 7/17

Philomeidêsion
Noumenia: 7/18
Deuteroebdomo: 7/25
Dichomenia: 8/1
Phthinontos: 8/8
Hene: 8/15
Hene kai Nea: 8/16

Sôteiraion
Noumenia: 8/17
Deuteroebdomo: 8/24
Dichomenia: 8/30
Phthinontos: 9/6
Hene kai Nea & Epistrophê: 9/14

Polyphrônion
Noumenia & Epistrophê: 9/15
Epistrophê: 9/16
Deuteroebdomo: 9/22
Dichomenia: 9/29
Phthinontos: 10/6
Hene kai Nea: 10/14

Agroterêion
Noumenia: 10/15
Deuteroebdomo: 10/21
Dichomenia: 10/28
Phthinontos: 11/5
Hene: 11/12
Hene kai Nea: 11/13

Diaktorosion
Noumenia: 11/14
Deuteroebdomo: 11/20
Dichomenia: 11/27
Phthinontos: 12/4
Hene kai Nea: 12/12

Khrysopêlêxion
Noumenia: 12/13
Deuteroebdomo: 12/19
Dichomenia: 12/26
Phthinontos: 1/3/24
Hene & Mone: 1/10
Hene kai Nea & Mone: 1/11

2024

Phyxiosion
Noumenia & Mone: 1/12/24
Mone: 1/13-14
Deuteroebdomo: 1/17
Dichomenia: 1/25
Phthinontos: 2/2
Hene kai Nea: 2/9

Hôrêphorosion
Noumenia: 2/10
Deuteroebdomo: 2/16
Dichomenia: 2/24
Phthinontos: 3/3
Hene: 3/19
Hene kai Nea: 3/10

Ouliosion
Noumenia: 3/11
Deuteroebdomo: 3/16
Dichomenia: 3/24
Phthinontos: 4/3
Hene kai Nea: 4/8

Escharaion
Noumenia: 4/9
Deuteroebdomo: 4/15
Dichomenia: 4/23
Phthinontos: 5/1
Hene kai Nea & Prohodos: 5/7

Ennosigaiosion
Noumenia & Prohodos: 5/8
Prohodos: 5/9
Deuteroebdomo: 5/15
Dichomenia: 5/23
Phthinontos: 5/30
Hene: 6/5
Hene kai Nea: 6/6

Antheiaion
Noumenia: 6/7
Deuteroebdomo: 6/14
Dichomenia: 6/21
Phthinontos: 6/28
Hene kai Nea: 7/5

Philomeidêsion
Noumenia: 7/6
Deuteroebdomo: 7/13
Dichomenia: 7/21
Phthinontos: 7/27
Hene: 8/3
Hene kai Nea: 8/4

Sôteiraion
Noumenia: 8/5
Deuteroebdomo: 8/12
Dichomenia: 8/19
Phthinontos: 8/26
Hene kai Nea & Epistrophê: 9/2

Polyphrônion
Noumenia & Epistrophê: 9/3
Epistrophê: 9/4
Deuteroebdomo: 9/11
Dichomenia: 9/17
Phthinontos: 9/24
Hene kai Nea: 10/2

Agroterêion
Noumenia: 10/3
Deuteroebdomo: 10/10
Dichomenia: 10/17
Phthinontos: 10/24
Hene: 10/31
Hene kai Nea: 11/1

Diaktorosion
Noumenia: 11/2
Deuteroebdomo: 11/8
Dichomenia: 11/15
Phthinontos: 11/22
Hene: 11/30
Hene kai Nea: 12/1

Khrysopêlêxion
Noumenia: 12/2
Deuteroebdomo: 12/8
Dichomenia: 12/15
Fthinonto: 12/22
Hene & Mone: 12/29
Hene kai Nea & Mone: 12/30

2025

Phyxiosion
Noumenia & Mone: 12/31
Mone: 1/1/25-1/2-25
Deuteroebdomo: 1/6
Dichomenia: 1/13
Phthinontos: 1/21
Hene: 1/28
Hene kai Nea: 1/29

Hôrêphorosion
Noumenia: 1/30
Deuteroebdomo: 2/5
Dichomenia: 2/12
Phthinontos: 2/20
Hene kai Nea: 2/27

Ouliosion
Noumenia: 2/28
Deuteroebdomo: 3/6
Dichomenia: 3/14
Phthinontos: 3/22
Hene: 3/28
Hene kai Nea: 3/29

Escharaion
Noumenia: 3/30
Deuteroebdomo: 4/4
Dichomenia: 4/12
Phthinontos: 4/20
Hene kai Nea & Prohodos: 4/27

Ennosigaiosion
Noumenia & Prohodos: 4/28
Prohodos: 4/29
Deuteroebdomo: 5/4

Dichomenia: 5/12
Phthinontos: 5/20
Hene kai Nea: 5/26

Antheiaion
Noumenia: 5/27
Deuteroebdomo: 6/2
Dichomenia: 6/11
Phthinontos: 6/18
Hene: 6/24
Hene kai Nea: 6/25

Philomeidêsion
Noumenia: 6/26
Deuteroebdomo: 7/2
Dichomenia: 7/10
Phthinontos: 7/17
Hene kai Nea: 7/24

Sôteiraion
Noumenia: 7/25
Deuteroebdomo: 8/1
Dichomenia: 8/9
Phthinontos: 8/16
Hene: 8/22
Hene kai Nea & Epistrophê: 8/23

Polyphrônion
Noumenia & Epistrophê: 8/24
Epistrophê: 8/25
Deuteroebdomo: 8/31
Dichomenia: 9/7
Phthinontos: 9/14
Hene kai Nea: 9/21

Agroterêion
Noumenia: 9/22
Deuteroebdomo: 9/29
Dichomenia: 10/6
Phthinontos: 10/13
Hene: 10/20
Hene kai Nea: 10/21

Diaktorosion
Noumenia: 10/22
Deuteroebdomo: 10/29
Dichomenia: 11/5
Phthinontos: 11/11
Hene: 11/19
Hene kai Nea: 11/20

Khrysopêlêxion
Noumenia: 11/21
Deuteroebdomo: 11/28
Dichomenia: 12/4
Fthinonto: 12/11
Hene kai Nea & Mone: 12/19

Nekrodegmônion
Noumenia & Henosi: 12/20
Henosi: 12/21
Deuteroebdomo: 12/27
Dichomenia: 1/3/26
Fthinonto: 1/10
Mone: 1/17
Hene kai Nea & Mone: 1/18

2026

Phyxiosion
Noumenia & Mone: 1/19
Mone: 1/20/-1/21
Deuteroebdomo: 1/25
Dichomenia: 2/1
Phthinontos: 2/9
Hene: 2/16
Hene kai Nea: 2/17

Hôrêphorosion
Noumenia: 2/18
Deuteroebdomo: 2/24
Dichomenia: 3/3
Phthinontos: 3/11
Hene kai Nea: 3/18

Ouliosion
Noumenia: 3/19
Deuteroebdomo: 3/25
Dichomenia: 4/1
Phthinontos: 4/9
Hene: 4/15
Hene kai Nea: 4/16

Escharaion
Noumenia: 4/17
Deuteroebdomo: 4/23
Dichomenia: 5/1
Phthinontos: 5/9
Hene kai Nea & Prohodos: 5/16

Ennosigaiosion
Noumenia & Prohodos: 5/17
Prohodos: 5/18
Deuteroebdomo: 5/23
Dichomenia: 5/31
Phthinontos: 6/8
Hene kai Nea: 6/14

Antheiaion
Noumenia: 6/15
Deuteroebdomo: 6/21
Dichomenia: 6/29
Phthinontos: 7/7
Hene: 7/13
Hene kai Nea: 7/14

Philomeidêsion
Noumenia: 7/15
Deuteroebdomo: 7/21
Dichomenia: 7/29
Phthinontos: 8/5
Hene kai Nea: 8/12

Sôteiraion
Noumenia: 8/13
Deuteroebdomo: 8/19
Dichomenia: 8/27
Phthinontos: 9/4
Hene kai Nea & Epistrophê: 9/10

Polyphrônion
Noumenia & Epistrophê: 9/11
Epistrophê: 9/12
Deuteroebdomo: 9/18
Dichomenia: 19/26
Phthinontos: 10/3
Hene: 10/9
Hene kai Nea: 10/10

Agroterêion
Noumenia: 10/11
Deuteroebdomo: 10/18
Dichomenia: 10/25
Phthinontos: 11/1
Hene: 11/8
Hene kai Nea: 11/9

Diaktorosion
Noumenia: 11/10
Deuteroebdomo: 11/17
Dichomenia: 11/24
Phthinontos: 12/1
Hene kai Nea: 12/8

Khrysopêlêxion
Noumenia: 12/9
Deuteroebdomo: 12/16
Dichomenia: 12/23
Fthinonto: 12/30
Hene: 1/6/27
Hene kai Nea & Mone: 1/7

Years with Intercalary Months through 2100

2028	2055	2082
2030	2058	2085
2033	2060	2087
2036	2063	2090
2039	2066	2093
2041	2068	2096
2044	2071	2098
2047	2074	2101
2049	2077	
2052	2079	

YEARLY HIEROMENIAS

Yearly Hieromenias

FOR AS WE ACKNOWLEDGE THE WORLD TO BE FULL OF MANY GOODS AND ALSO OF EVILS, AND OF MORE EVILS THAN GOODS, THERE IS, AS WE AFFIRM, AN IMMORTAL CONFLICT GOING ON AMONG US, WHICH REQUIRES MARVELOUS WATCHFULNESS; AND IN THAT CONFLICT THE GODS AND DEMI-GODS ARE OUR ALLIES, AND WE ARE THEIR PROPERTY. INJUSTICE AND INSOLENCE AND FOLLY ARE THE DESTRUCTION OF US, AND JUSTICE AND TEMPERANCE AND WISDOM ARE OUR SALVATION; AND THE PLACE OF THESE LATTER IS IN THE LIFE OF THE GODS, ALTHOUGH SOME VESTIGE OF THEM MAY OCCASIONALLY BE DISCERNED AMONG HUMANKIND.

PLATO, LAWS, X. 906A

Laws Quotation for Seasons

Pythagoras

CHAPTER 5

Prayer Services for the Yearly Hieromenias

PRAYER SERVICE FOR THE OBSERVATION OF MONE

Celebrant: *(three times)* Worshippers of the gods give ear. This is the hour for the Dew [or Noontide or Evensong] prayer. Let us invoke all the divinities and the holy Demiurgos, who reigns over them, with all our mind, and all our reason, and all our soul.[75]

All kneel on both knees, facing the same direction.[76] Everyone makes the gesture of invocation: arms raised and held outwards, with palms up.

All: O divine ones, be propitious.[77]

Raise one knee, touch the ground with the right hand.

All: O divine ones, be propitious.

Lift right hand, touch the ground with the left hand.

All: O divine ones, be propitious.

Make full prostration: both knees, hands, and forehead touching the ground.

All: *(three times)* O Demiurgos, be propitious.

---

[75] Alternatively: "with all our essence, our all power, and all our activity." All of the prayers here are written in the plural but can be changed to the singular with difficulty.
[76] Plethon does not specify a direction, or no such specification has survived to my knowledge. Use whichever direction is appropriate to your overall ritual praxis.
[77] Alternatively: "O gods, be propitious" or "O God, be propitious."

Boreas

The Hour of Dew Prayer

Hail to you, glorious First-Born of the shock-white hair!

Great and endless Lord, who stands alone above all, we call to you!

Holy Eternity, though beyond essence, be present to us this hour.

O Lord without beginning or end, you were great before all, and without you, all is naught.

It was you who caused the Thunderbolt to show mercy to humanity,

And it was you who held together the bonds of creation at the will of the King of Heaven through the deluge.

Hearken, O Eternity, and hold us that we do not slip into chaos.

Guide the ways of our feet that we do not step off the precipice into the light-hating world.

Be always with us, Father of Essence, so we do not falter.

The Noontide Prayers and Hymns

O you, who are girt 'round by the seven-fold serpent and twelve living creatures, hear our prayer.

Mighty king who encompasses all of knowledge from above, give heed to our cry!

Listen to our plea, you imageless one before the dawn of thought.

Before the Beginning was you, and after all has passed you will remain.

And it was you, in unsurpassable glory, who filled the cosmos with air and set the sun in motion.

Your child is Time, and your image is the Soul of the World.

Through your children let the world below be known.

Lift us up, Paternal Intellect, that we may gaze into heaven, and through heaven, Eternity.

Awaken the flower of our souls, Holy Eternity, that by your hand we may be free.

Hearken, great and holy First-Born,
*   Golden-winged glorious one!*
O you Father of Essences,
*   Lion-headed, unseen sun*
Who plucks the high flower of Mind.
*   Imageless Lord, heed our cry,*
Raise us to your infinite height,
*   That your Goodness may be nigh.*

You about whom the serpent coils,
  Impart Intellect to us
That we may perceive true Goodness.
  Through your faith, not in the truss
Of the coiling serpent or the
  Sphere of circling creatures,
Settle our gaze upon your light
  And your imageless features.

Hearken, Intellect thinking himself, listen to our holy cry.
Be with us in this hour, O God of Gods.
Mark our words, You who are above the heavens.
You hold the Key to All in your right hand and in your left is writ the Word of creation.
For your Word is an offspring of Light who glorifies your invisible form,
And all the heavens quake at its sounding.
Open to us, O Lord, the path of Faith that we may enter therein,
And, through your knowledge, know ourselves.
Through you, let us perceive the Good Itself.

First act of magic, Creator
  Before creation, Monad
Of the intelligible realm,
  Self-generated comrade
To our souls: O great one!
  Child of the Good, admit
Us to the mysteries of faith
  That our souls be not unfit.

Awaken our souls, O great Lord,
  You Good Spirit and Father,
That we may heed the words of the

Oracle without bother
Or tribulation. You bade the
  Orderer towards mercy,
Now show mercy to us, O Lord.
  O First One, grant us this plea.

To you we pray, who was before the Word that sounded through creation.
You, who are self-begotten, the first Moment of the intelligible, hear our cry.
O God of Gods, fill us with your own power, listen to our prayer.
To you belonged the cosmos before it was filled with essence.
Before the heavens arose, you knit the firmament together,
And it was you who were before duality arose, too.
Through your Moments let us know ourselves as we truly are,
And so follow the words of the Philosopher, and become like God, so far as possible.
Holy Eternity, we seek through you knowledge of the highest, you who encompasses the Craftsmen in your hand.

The Evensong Prayer

O holy perpetual Time, highest Principle after the Unknowable, we pray to you.
Hear us, O Great King who is unrolled in an eternal circle.
Listen to our cry, O Everlasting Father of Demiurges.
Before the beginning you stood above the chaos, and because of you there will be no end.
Intelligible life of the Simply One, you hold the entirety of the divine intellect in your hands.
You are the soundless voice of the unknowable Father, and forever is but a moment to your eternity.
Let this season of Remaining bring us closer to you, O Intelligible Source of Being.
Through Remaining let us know the series to which we belong.
Hear our prayer, Holy Eternity, so your providence rains down upon us.

Readings for Lectio Divina

Gods, children of gods, who are my works and of whom I am the artificer and father, my creations are indissoluble, if I so will. – Plato, *Timaeus*, 41a.

All that is bound may be undone, but only an evil being would wish to undo that which is harmonious and happy. – Plato, *Timaeus*, 41b.

…the allotments of the gods do indeed stand eternal…. - Iamblichus, *In Tim*, fr. 14.

And further basing this narration on the sacred writings, which shows the permanent watch of the cosmic divine forms…. – Iamblichus, *In Tim*, fr. 14A.

The Demiurge sows [souls] among all the superior classes, throughout all the heavens, and into all the elements of the universe. – Iamblichus, *De Anima*, VI.A.26.377.15-18.

Every productive cause produces the next and all subsequent principles while itself remaining steadfast. – Proclus, *Elements of Theology*, §26.

All that is immediately produced by any principle both remains in the producing cause and proceeds from it. – Proclus, *Elements of Theology*, §30.

PRAYER SERVICE FOR THE OBSERVATION OF PROHODOS

The Hour of Dew Prayer

Hail to you, eternal eye that sees all the Earth!

Golden Lord, who sets the heavens in order, we call to you!

Holy King of Heaven and Earth, most holy Craftsman, be present to us in this hour.

O Lord of intellective flames, your approach chases away night and chaos.

It was you who, O Eye of Justice, who set the ways upon which we travel in our orbits.

And it was you who spoke the Words which set our souls in motion.

Hearken, O Lord of the horizon, and do not let us lose our way.

Guide us so we may sow your freedom wherever we walk.

Be always with us, Saviour and watchman, so we may shape your kingdom in the image of truth.

The Noontide Prayers and Hymns

O you, Seven-Rayed King who rules over the seven zones, hear our prayer.

Mighty Sovereign, whose word sets all in motion, give heed to our cry!

Listen to our plea, you whose gaze pierces every darkness.

Before the glory of the day, you rest in the eternal ocean.

And it was you, in blinding brilliance, who lights our way with heavenly fire.

Your children are the glory of day, twelve stations by which we mark your passage.

Through your children let divine illumination be known to us.

Lift us up, Divine Knowledge, that we may rejoin our series around its heavenly course.

Awaken our minds, holy giver of freedom, that we may set our wills aright.

Hearken, illuminating King
*   Of the luminous seven*
Rays! Blinding Gleam with aureole
*   Fine, lead us up to heaven.*
King of Heaven and Earth, brilliant
*   Orderer and creator,*
Set us in our orbit's motion
*   To a realm that is greater.*

Zephyros

You who give the cosmos order,
  Let us partake of your Mind
So we may better know ourselves
  And no longer be so blind
To our true natures. Let your truth
  Open our eyes and make clear
Our paths. Let evil be without
  Dominion in your bright sphere.

Hearken, Divine Gleam who travels high paths, listen to our holy cry.
Be with us in this hour, Lord of the two horizons.
Mark our words, Averter of Evil.
You hold Power in your right hand, and in your left is the Sign of Life.
For your Word is the boundary between above and below,
And all the worlds listen to your ordering speech.
Open to us, O far-seeing one, our heavenly circuit that we may return home,
And through your Word we may create in your image.
Through you, let divine knowledge be open to us.

Intellective King, hear this song
  To your glory! Radiant
All-seeing eye of splendour, you
  Mighty lord of the brilliant
Horizons, be here in your strength!
  Stretch out your right hand and show
Us your ways, stretch out your left so
  The immortal life does flow.

It is you who sets us on our
  Journey, the heavenly way
Which always leads back home. Keep us

safe, let us not go astray.
O blinding guard, Divine Mind,
Bright reflection of the Good,
Let us match your glory and help
Us to shape this world of wood.

To you we pray, King of All, the Word of creation.
You who protect all wisdom and truth, hear our cry.
O Leader of the Heavens, listen to our prayer.
To you belongs the heavens and the Earth.
Before the divine circuits were established, you commanded that they be.
And it was you who gave the divinities their tasks above and below.
Through following our circuits we proceed from heaven to Earth,
And so following the prompting of our souls, which proceed with your reason.
Holy Divine Radiance, we seek through you the illuminated path which leads always to your domain.

The Evensong Prayer

O holy and radiant King, through whose light we mark the hours of our lives, we pray to you.
Hear us, O Giver of Life, who describes morning and night.
Listen to our cry, O Divine Intellect, ruler of Heaven and Earth.
Before the light of the sun arose, you shone in the celestial sky, and you lead us away from your home as we seek
you.
Intellective Mind of the heavenly realm, your brilliance sets the truth before us on our path.
You are the Word of unspoken Eternity, and through you we see all that is Good.
Let this season of Procession bring us closer to knowing our place in the cosmos, O Creative Mind.
Through Procession let our experiences lead us to fullness.
Hear our prayer, Holy King of All, so we may better know your domain, which you have granted to us as your
vice-regents.

Readings for Lectio Divina

Around the hollow of her right flank a great stream of the primordially-generated Soul gushes forth in abundance, totally ensouling light, fire, ether, worlds. – *Chaldean Oracles*, fr. 51.3-5.

From there, the birth of variegated matter leaps forth. – *Chaldean Oracles*, fr. 34.3.

For indeed the philosopher is a sophist inasmuch as he imitates both the heavenly Demiurge and the demiurge who presided over generation. – Iamblichus, *In Soph*, fr. I.13-16.

The Dyad [is] the organizer of Procession and Division. – Iamblichus, *In Tim*, fr. 53.8-9.

He calls the Ogdoad the cause of Procession to all points and of Progression through all… – Iamblichus, *In Tim*, fr. 53.14.

For it is said to be formed by the art of the Demiurge himself. – Iamblichus, *De Mysteriis*, III.28.168.13-14.

Notos

PRAYER SERVICE FOR THE OBSERVATION OF EPISTROPHE

The Hour of Dew Prayer

Hail to you, mighty saviour of souls!

Great and frenzied lord, who was divided for our sake!

Holy Ruler of the Living Souls, who heals what was sundered, be present to us this hour!

O Lord of images, you alone judge deeds obscure and conspicuous, no soul may hide from you.

It was you who fed us on our journey, making the Earth abundant.

And it was you who caused us to forget our origins, so we might remember through our own power.

Hearken, Master of Daimons, and do not let us become mired in your darkly splendid world.

Guide our minds towards their origins, let us not be straight but bent in divine orbit.

Be always with us, host of multitudes, that we may return to our places in heaven.

The Noontide Prayers and Hymns

O you, saviour of the whole world, whose key unlocks the gates of the Earth, hear our prayer.

Mighty ruler of the multitudes, who frees souls from error, give heed to our cry!

Listen to our plea, you who purifies souls from the accretions of mistaken paths.

Before the endless gate, you set guards along the way.

And it is you, in dark splendour, who judges all souls standing between this world and that.

Your children bring an end to all in the world so we may rise to the world above.

Through your children let us one day know the name of our soul.

Lift us up, even in this life, and let us open the Daimon Gate to self-knowledge.

Awaken the words of our souls, that the wrong may be separated from the right.

Hail to you great King beneath the
*   Moon's hallowed glow. O Saviour*
Of fractured souls, lead us towards
*   Our home. Lord of Daimons, spur*
Us onwards so we may return
*   Along our orbit's long course*

To our heavenly abode. O
  Great King, send us to our source.

Hearken, you who liberates souls,
  Listen to our hymn. Do not
Let us remain in darkness but
  Bring us instead to that spot
Which raises souls to perfection.
  Separate from us all which
Is averse to virtue, set our
  Harmony to perfect pitch.

Hearken, Frenzied God who separates divine proportions, listen to our holy cry.
Be with us in this hour, Bringer of Liberation.
Mark our words, you who were uplifted on golden wings.
You hold seeds and honey in your right hand, and from your left drips the liquor of dissolution.
For your Word divides what is like from what is different,
And all the Earth is touched by your liberating hand.
Open to us, O Bringer of Mysteries, that we may be divided and made anew,
And through your frenzy may we be made free from chaff.
Through you, may all our proportions be made right.

Great Hunter of souls, free us from
  the dregs of illusion, bring
us to where we may cast off what
  is untrue, where we may fling
away that which is impure in
  us. Frenzied and divided
God, dissolve the chains that bind us
  to this place we have long trod.

Healer of souls, perfector of
  Proportions, place your strong hand
upon our heads, make whole what is
  now divided. Let us stand
before the divinities in
  perfect harmony, many
made one just as one becomes the
  many. Great Lord, hear our plea.

To you we pray, Soothing Lord, who heals all errors of body and soul.
You who love all the people of the Earth, hear our cry.
O Purifier of Souls, listen to our prayer.
To you belongs the power which restores that which was sundered.
Before the soul's descent, you knew the proportions of our beings.
And it is you who speaks the words that raise us from the earthly grave.
Through your will we mortals are brought immortal joy
And so once more return home without fault or blemish.
Holy and Supreme Authority, we seek through you our perfection that we may participate the source of perfection.

The Evensong Prayer

O holy and many-headed Creator, we pray to you.
Hear us, O Image-Maker, who with sorcery shapes and divides and puts together once more.
Listen to our cry, you Purifier of Souls.
Before the end of our lives you set us in proportion, even if against the life we have, in our error, mis-chosen for
  ourselves.
Generative and sub-lunar King, you are the sun at midnight, guiding our way even in darkness.
You are the action of the Word made manifest, and through you we are healed and made holy.
Let this season of Reversion guide us back to our orbits, let us not remain lost.
Through Reversion let us become fully ourselves, and like God, so far as possible.

Hear our prayer, Holy King of this darkly splendid world, not that we may escape this world, but that we may raise it to perfection.

Readings for Lectio Divina

So it appears that when death comes to a man, the mortal part of him dies, but the immortal part retires at the approach of death and escapes unharmed and indestructible. – Plato, *Phaedo*, 106e.

[S]ince the soul is clearly immortal, it can have no escape or security from evil except by becoming as good and wise as it possibly can. – Plato, *Phaedo*, 107c-d.

Grant that I may become fair within, and that such outward things as I have may not war against the spirit within me. – Plato, *Phaedrus*, 279b.

Let us consider the following as the most useful of all the ends of the purification: removal of foreign elements, restoration of one's own essence, perfection, fulfilment, self-sufficiency, ascent to the engendering cause, conjoining of parts to whole, and the gift of power, life, and activity from wholes to individuals. – Iamblichus, *De Anima*, VIII.A.43.456.1.5.[78]

Plato's *Timaeus*, however, elevates them in their ascent even as they were sown variously by the Demiurge, some into the Sun, others into the Earth... – Iamblichus, *De Anima*, VIII.B.49.457.15-16.

Every effect remains in its cause, proceeds from it, and reverts upon it. – Proclus, *Elements of the Theology*, §35.

---

[78] *It may be beneficial to choose only one or two of the ends listed rather than the whole list.*

PRAYER SERVICE FOR THE OBSERVATION OF HENOSI

The Hour of Dew Prayer

Hail to you, mighty and eternal spirit!

Great and good daimon who lives above, between, and within, we call to you!

Holy protector, crowned with glory and supernal wisdom, be present to us this hour.

O Lord of our past, present, and future, you stood before the heavens were formed, and wrapped yourself around the World Soul.

It was you who set the heavens in motion, giving them order when there was only chaos,

And it was you who guided our steps towards holiness.

Hearken, O saviour of all our lives, past and present, incline towards us the graces.

Guide our minds towards heavenly reunion.

Be always with us, divine goodness, so we may know blessings here and above.

The Noontide Prayers and Hymns

O you, Lord who is wrapped in quarters around our souls, hear our prayer.

Mighty Guardian, who secures for us every blessing, give heed to our cry!

Listen to our plea, O you who teaches us every lesson and corrects our every mistake.

Before we were born you guided us and in our ignorance goaded us forward.

And it was you to whom our souls were given when sown into their heavenly orbits.

Your children are we who kneel before you that your blessings and knowledge may rain upon us.

Through your children let the world be set in order.

Lift us up to our divine glory in heaven and over the Earth.

Awaken our true names that we may speak your praise.

Hail to you holy daimon and
*   Sacred guide. Divine Power*
We raise our words to you, Urger
*   Towards heaven, who does stir*
In us an upwards yearning to
*   Divine ends. Most sacred friend*
And prompter towards Goodness, point
*   The way and help us ascend.*

Euros

O you most holy parent and
   Sovereign benefactor:
You have watched us since we first fell
   From heaven and now do spur
Us to find our homes. So do now
   Aid us to regain our way
And to find our bearings. Lead us
   So we do not go astray.

Hearken mighty daimon, Good and guardian spirit, listen to our holy cry.
Be with us in this hour, mighty Authority guiding our souls.
Mark our words, you who urge us towards the Divine.
You hold the way to the perfection of our souls in your right hand, and in your left the key to the gateway of the
   Divine Intellect.
For your Word sends us, willing or not, into incarnation,
And all under your power must heed your prompting.
Open to us, you who are from the entire cosmos, our eyes that we may see ourselves truly,
And through your divinely gifted sight, let us know ourselves.
Through you, let us move in circular fashion, to become like God, so far as possible.

We lift our song to you, holy
   Companion and salvation.
Guardian of souls, to you we
   Sing at the height of the sun.
The reins slipped from our hands and you
   Steadied us. The steed rebelled
And it was you who gentled us
   Down until its temper quelled.

Sacred guardian, correct us
   In our error that we may

Know the vessel from its pilot.
  Set us upon the broad way
And the vast sea of the heavens
  That the helmsman may steer the
Ship towards its rightful shore so
  The divine song we may hear.

To you we pray, mighty and divine Power, harbinger of the Divine.
You who guide our feet, even when we reject the holy ways, hear our cry.
O guardian of souls, listen to our prayer.
To you belongs the days and nights of our lives until we walk as adults with the souls of babes.
Before our birth you knew us, and you directed us towards that which is best.
And it is you who corrects us when we fail, and rejoices with us when we succeed.
Through holy providence we will know you and rise upwards towards the heavens,
And so again become established in our orbits.
Holy Guardian and Guide, we seek through you that which is higher. Set us on our path.

The Evensong Prayer

O holy guardian and divine guide, we pray to you.
Hear us, O you who is appointed over us from on high.
Listen to our cry, mighty daimon and soul's friend.
Before we were born you guided us towards life, and as we grow in this life, and leave it, you are here for us.
Guide and holy counsel, it is by you we may arise to our divinely appointed glory.
You are the hand that steadies us, the guide that directs us, the hope that nourishes us, and the lead that corrects
    us.
Let this season of contemplation bring us closer to you.
Through contemplation let us realize our holiness that divine holiness may be realized through us.
Hear our prayer, Holy Power and Authority, so we may heed the Oracle and know ourselves.

Readings for Lectio Divina

O King, you have brought to light divine works. – *Orphic Hymns*, 'To Zeus,' 3-5.

The leader of the celestial gods, whom [Hermes] declares to be an intellect thinking himself… – Iamblichus, *De Mysteriis*, VIII.3.263.1-3.

It is in [Heikton] that there resides the primal intelligising element and the primal object of intellection, which… is worshipped by means of silence alone. – Iamblichus, *De Mysteriis*, VIII.3.263.45.

This daimon, then, stands as a model for us even before the souls descend into generation. – Iamblichus, *De Mysteriis*, IX.6.280.6-8.

LUNAR HIEROMENIAS

Lunar Hieromenias

hen the father creator
saw the creature which
he had made moving and
living, the created image
of the eternal gods, he
rejoiced, and in his joy determined
to make the copy still more like
the original; and as this was
eternal, he sought to make the
universe eternal, so far as might be.
Now the nature of the ideal being
was everlasting, but to bestow
this attribute in its fulness upon a
creature was impossible.

PLATO, TIMAEUS, 37D-E

Timaeus

Plato

CHAPTER 6

Prayer Services for the Lunar Hieromenias

PRAYER SERVICE FOR THE OBSERVATION OF NOUMENIA

The Hour of Dew Prayer

Hail Thunder, Perfect Mind: celestial orderer, hear our prayer!
Mighty King of All, who causes the movements of the moon, we call to you.
Hearken, O Saviour who gives light to the world in darkness.
Now is the time you set for beginnings, so we celebrate the new cycle.
Your light rises from the darkness as the dawn sings your praise.
Our day and month begins anew, and so you are celebrated, O source of our existence.
At this time of beginnings, purify our souls, O King, so we may live in your virtues.
Let our past faults be corrected, our errors set aside that we may walk in divine ways.
O Divine brilliance, lead us in holy ways as we set forth on our journey.

The Noontide Prayers and Hymns

We pray to you, O celestial Creator, leader of leaders, hear us.
Upon the holy Demiurgos we call, great lord of the heavens, be with us.
O Intellective Order, creator of all that is immortal, raise us unto you.
The pre-essential creator spoke, and you were His Word, singing through creation.
Your words echo through the heavens and Earth.
Your series separates odds and evens, putting all in their proper place.
Through you, let our allotment be ordered and perfected.
In us, let all the proper tokens and signs be assembled to fulfilment.
In your Name and words, let us govern with virtue and beauty.

New Moon

We raise our voices, mighty King,
  To your praise. Your Light perfects
All upon which it shines, and you
  Are one of the architects
Of the Heavens. In your orbit
  Lie division and union
And through these two is the divine
  Will brought into fruition.

Let your bright arrows pierce our minds
  And your series lift us up
That we may see you and know you,
  And that knowing develop
Into our fullest selves. Help us
  To resign from this great plight
That we may regain what has been
  Lost, our heavenly birthright.

Hear our prayer, O Protector of Truth, seven-rayed God.
We call to you, O Master of Wisdom, shaper of reason in the soul.
To you we speak praises, Lord of the Two Horizons, hearken unto us.
From heavenly heights you watch all the Earth, seeing everything in its place.
Where your rays shine, order reigns and Providence sings.
Where your lightning strikes, ignorance is obliterated and knowledge is grasped.
Let your Light shine upon us, O Lord, that we may live in your glory.
Through your enlightenment may we know all that is true and holy.
As we observe your heavenly course let us take part in the harmony of the cosmic motion.

O holy one, intellective
  Mind, we pray to you. Divine
King, mighty Craftsman, Leader of

All the heavens, do consign
To us the wisdom to stand in
* Your glory. Those in your train*
Set heaven and Earth in order
* So all revel in your reign.*

Through your unity all things strive
* To become one. From the One*
To the twelve to the seven then
* five more, the cosmos is done*
When below mirrors above and
* All settles to its proper*
Place. Our paths are set in your eyes,
* From them, do not let us stir.*

O Holy Craftsman, Divine Intellect and monad of the Whole Soul, we pray to you.
Great and noble Eye of the King, far-seeing guardian, hear us.
Most exalted ruler of Fate, you who are great in heaven, listen and be near.
In the heavens you set the duodecade in order and rule the hebdomad.
Each soul you sow into the orbit of one of the twelve, setting angel and spirit above them.
You direct each soul in its course, downwards and then back to you through its proper channel.
Grant us prosperity in each life until we return home.
Set in our paths your signs and tokens so we may never wander lost and alone.
Let us know you, great Mind, that through you we may know ourselves.

The Evensong Prayers

O Divine King of Heaven and Earth, hear our prayer.
Great King who causes the sun to set by your masterful design, we give you our praise.
Listen to our plea, O Leader of the Heavenly circuit, to whom all, at last, are reconciled.

You lead all around their appointed orbits, rising and setting in harmony: remaining, proceeding, and, at last, returning.
Your will supports the world, and by your goodness all divinities are made eternal, even as you
Have made our souls.
Through your holiness all are made perfect.
By your goodness, let our lives, step by step, be resolved in you.
Let our lives be fulfilled and, in fulfilment, a glory upon the diadem of heavenly stars.
This we pray as we seek the Good in which you so fully participate.

Readings for Lectio Divina

The part of them worthy of the name immortal, which is called divine and is the guiding principle of those who are willing to follow justice and you – of that divine part I will myself sow the seed… - Plato, *Timaeus*, 41e.

For Intellect derived from Intellect is the Craftsman of the fiery cosmos. – *Chaldean Oracles*, fr 5.

You gods who know the supermundane, Paternal Abyss by perceiving it. – *Chaldean Oracles*, fr. 18.

The Primary beings illuminate even the lowest levels, and the immaterial are present immaterially to the material. – Iamblichus, *De Mysteriis*, V.23.232.10-13.

[W]e speak of a pure and divine form of matter; for matter also issues from the Father and creator of all, and thus gains its perfection which is suitable to the reception of gods. – Iamblichus, *De Mysteriis*, V.23.232.13-233.2.

Waxing Half Moon

PRAYER SERVICE FOR THE OBSERVATION OF DEUTEROEBDOMO

Hour of Dew Prayer

Hail great daimons, guardians and nurturers of the generative realm, hear our prayer!

Mighty rulers of fate and land, you who are appointed a duty singular, we call to you.

Hearken, O Authorities, custodians of lands and families both.

Now is the time we give special honour to you, as you unerringly oversee your tasks.

Your glorious forms purify all who behold them.

Our prayers rise up to you, for you are honoured in your duties.

At this time of the yearly cycle, be present to us that we may guard from erring against your domains, now and for all times.

Let our paths lead us away from fault and righteous wrath.

O Divine Powers, let us not fall into error as we proceed through the cycles of the year.

The Noontide Prayers and Hymns

We pray to you, daimonic conductors of the generative realm, hear us.

Upon the spirits of the cosmos we call, spirits of a unique power, be with us.

O relational daimons, keepers of the Earth, be known to us.

The Creative Mind gave you your singular tasks, and you attend your duties without fail.

Your activities put the world in its proper order, like the circles of sameness and difference encircling the Soul, you make all things complete.

Your work enables us to live unhindered in our faith.

Through you we may do the work of the Creator.

In us lies the sacred words, which you put into order in this realm.

By your Names all things may be accomplished in the realm of generation.

We raise our voices to the great
Spirits of the world, holy
Conductors of all that must be
Done in generation. Sea
And sky and earth are set beneath

Your one task, and in sacred
Demiurgy we hasten to
Fulfil your acts undaunted.

O daimonic guardians and
Spiritual judges who
Protect the innocent and do
Correct those without virtue,
We hymn thee. Teach us to live in
Greatness, our lives devoted
To higher aims, even in this
Realm which you have so girded.

Hear our prayer, O daimonic guardians of what is good in this world.
We call to you, O great judges who see all things from above the fullness of time.
To you we speak praises, spirits who gives justice to the righteous and the unrighteous.
From encosmic heavens you watch the actions of all humanity, guarding, adjudicating, and acting in accordance
with Fate.
Where your place in the world is set, harmony reigns.
Where your advice is given, knowledge and virtue flourish.
Let your words be clear to us and lead us in the ways of justice.
Through your guidance let us sink not down into this fleshy world.
As we observe your divine ways, help us to participate in their glory.

To guardian daimons we sing,
You keepers of sanctity.
With manifold names you guard and
Guide places of chastity
And virtue, moving us to do
What is right, correcting us

When we lose the path. Holy ones,
Do you rightly guide us thus.

Most holy daimon set over
Our souls, with this song we praise
You. We are set in your orbit
And in heeding you we raise
Ourselves to know what is above.
Divinity, take us in
Hand and lead us and fill our days
With holiness from within.

O mighty Daimon, whom the Craftsman has set over us, we pray to you.
Great authority over each soul in your care, hear us.
Most exalted guide who watches us before, during, and after each life, listen and be near.
In the heavens you guard and guide the soul set before you without err.
Each soul you keep so, even without knowing you, it walks the path to self-knowledge.
You direct all within your care, celebrating our victories and when we stray from the path.
Grant us knowledge of yourself that we might know you better.
Set in our paths all which will help us rise to divine heights.
Let us know you, let your Name resound in our ears, that through you we might become One.

The Evensong Prayers

O Divine Spirits set over nature, hear our prayer.
Great daimons who lead souls in their circuits, we give you our praise.
Listen to our plea, O guardians of place and virtue.
You, in your simplicity, guide the elements of generation to fruition.
Your foresight directs each soul to their proper place upon the way of procession.
Through your intellective wisdom, you judge all according to their virtues.
By your activities, let our Earthly lives be in accordance with nature's dictates.

Let our journeys into multiplicity and back be swift and fortuitous.
This we pray as we seek to be made perfect in the divine image.

Readings for Lectio Divina

It is not from matter nor from the elements nor from any other body known to us that the body-like vehicle that serves daimons is composed. – Iamblichus, *De Mysteriis*, V.12.215.6-8.

Daimons assume guardianship over the arcane mysteries, because... they primarily contain the orderly arrangement in the world. – Iamblichus, *De Mysteriis*, VI.7.247.13-248.1.

The personal daimon [is] from the whole cosmos and from the whole variety of life within it... – Iamblichus, *De Mysteriis*, IX.6.280.1-4.

This daimon, then, stands as a model for us even before the souls descend into generation. – Iamblichus, *De Mysteriis*, IX.6.280.6-7.

For the personal daimon does not guide just one or another part of our being, but all of them at once. – Iamblichus, *De Mysteriis*, IX.7.281.6-7.

PRAYER SERVICE FOR THE OBSERVATION OF DICHOMENIA

Hour of Dew Prayer

Hail great heroes, defenders of our souls, hear our prayer!

Mighty protectors, divine and virtuous ones, we call to you.

Hearken, great messengers from the heavens.

Now is the time when we give homage to all great heroes as you labour to improve our souls.

Your manners direct us towards courage, your beauty towards wisdom. Help us fulfil ourselves with temperance and justice.

Our lives are illuminated by yours, our souls driven towards virtue.

At this time, the most fortuitous of moments of the lunar orbit, set us upon noble ways through your examples.

Let your glory lead us on to new heights.

O Divine guardians, brilliant beyond the soul's kin, be forever in advance that we might follow your ways.

The Noontide Prayers and Hymns

We pray to you, great protectors of Virtue, hear us.

Upon the Heroes who spur us on to noble deeds we call, be with us.

O supreme messengers of the divine orders, raise us unto you.

The heads of the duodecad set you amongst us to teach us Virtue through great actions.

Your activities give life, purity, and order to our souls.

Your presence stirs in us the desire to become more than what we are.

Through you we rise to accomplish the work of the perfection of the soul.

In us you stir noble urges and right livelihood.

By your many names and stories, be a model to us that we know an unspotted life.

Hail to the great ones! We praise you
*   And your great, valorous lives.*
Mighty Heroes, you teach us the
*   Way of virtue, which arrives*
In our hearts with honour and strength.
*   Hear our humble prayers. Lead us*
Forward in life. Make us wise, brave,
*   And mild beneath your aegis.*

Full Moon

Most holy messengers of life
  Made virtuous, who by your
Examples lead us to greatness
  Of word and deed. Your allure
Raises men and women to acts
  Of valour, keeping with what
Is right before the divine that
  Upon shame we do not glut.

Hear our prayer, O great Sons and Daughters of the Divine!
We call to you, O Heroes of word and deed.
To you we speak praises, you of courageous beauty and valour.
From virtuous heights you encourage us to match your greatness.
Where your activities manifest the virtues are increased.
Where your nobility touches us, we rise to become more like you.
Let your deeds be as beacons for us, directing us towards even greater heights.
Through your stories let us avoid hubris.
As we observe your lives in myth and song, guide us towards a virtuous life.

Exalted children of divine
  Nobility, we sing to
You who have shown us righteousness
  And the consequences due
Those who do not walk its great ways,
  To do you we give thanks. Let
Your example lead us away
  From base hubris and foul debt.

You have been placed in the heavens
  As signs for us to follow.
Help us see your tokens clearly

So that we can better grow
In virtue. Let our doings and
   Lives be worthy of greatness.
That through them we may better know
   You, and through you be blameless.

O high messengers of virtue, we pray to you.
Great exemplars of nobility, hear us.
Most exalted Heroes, children of the divine, progenitors great in stature, listen and be near.
In the heavens you have been given a place for the greatness of your lives.
Each soul that witnesses your activities rises to imitate examples you set.
You direct all of humanity to greatness of deed and word and virtue.
Grant us vitality that life comes to all our endeavours.
Set in our paths challenges worthy of our lives.
Let us know you that we might participate through you the heights of virtue.

The Evensong Prayers

O magnificent ones, glorious and munificent heroes, hear our prayer.
Great warriors, clever speakers, wise councillors, gifted of the divine, we give you our praise.
Listen to our plea, O messengers of virtue who have demonstrated to us the noble life, and even nobility's failure.
You have set examples for all to follow, glorifying wisdom, bravery, temperance, and justice.
Your deeds have inspired generations and will bring insight to generations to come.
Through your lives we are brought to the heights of generation.
By your lives let us live in participation of human, and divine, merit.
Let our lives be guided by your exemplars.
This we pray as we seek to mould ourselves in the image of the heavenly virtue.

Readings for Lectio Divina

The unexamined life is not worth living. – Plato, *Apology*, 38a.

Heroes… receive… unity and purity and permanent stability, undivided identity and transcendence over other things. – Iamblichus, *De Mysteriis*, I.6.19.11-20.2.

Heroes are produced according to the principles of life among the gods… – Iamblichus, *De Mysteriis*, II.1.67.5-6.

[The nature of] heroes is full of life and reason, and has leadership over souls. – Iamblichus, *De Mysteriis*, II.1.67.11-12.

The advent of heroes… is distinctive in arousing us to noble and great deeds. – Iamblichus, *De Mysteriis*, II.6.82.11-12.

Let courage… be understood to be such as is an unshakable intellectual potency, and the highest form of intellectual activity… – Iamblichus, 'On Courage,' Letter X, fr 1.1-2.

Waning Half Moon

PRAYER SERVICE FOR THE OBSERVATION OF PHTHINONTOS

Hour of Dew Prayer

Hail to you, the sacred dead, those who have come before and will come again, hear our prayer!

Mighty messengers of the divine, come to us who are stamped with the same divine image, for we call to you.

Hearken to us, O you, our sacred lineages.

Now is the time to fully celebrate your place in our lives, for where you are we will one day be.

Your presence causes the purification of souls, like calling to like.

Our lives will follow your holy ways, raising us up into holiness.

At this time, be you present to us, your visible light shining from heavenly glory.

Let your wisdom guide us in our orbits.

O ancestral guardians, images of the divine, help us to walk always in that sacred splendour.

The Noontide Prayers and Hymns

We pray to you, ancestors who have come before us and who we will one day join, hear us.

Upon the daimons who guide our families we call to you, the sacred dead, be with us.

O holy ones, purified souls, forbearers and progenitors, raise us to you.

The underworldly Lord has set you in your places, according to your virtues.

Your series sets you in your proper orbit, governing generation according to your principles.

Your daimons have guided you to purity, let your return here be by your will alone.

Through you we have come to this place, at this time, help us to live in purity as you have done.

In us, let your holiness manifest until you return to complete your work.

By your names and images, help us to achieve all that you have.

We lift our voices to you, O
   Sacred dead, ancestral source:
Hear our hymn. You purified ones,
   Forbearers, let your discourse
Make us aware of higher realms
   And let your good presence bring

Happiness and comfort in this
   Life, and beauty without sting.

And to the Lovers of Wisdom
   Who have come before, we sing.
Let your words inspire us, O
   Holy ones, so that nothing
May prevent us from looking where
   You have pointed: true knowledge
Of the heavens. Philosopher
   We listen with no umbrage.

Hear our prayers, wise you souls who have shown us the way to understanding.
We call to you, great souls who have come before us and shown us the way home.
To you we speak praises, the holy and sacred Philosophers who have affixed your eyes on a goal divine.
From your heavenly circuit you have come into generation to guide the multitudes, transforming the many into one.
Where you have spoken, those who love wisdom have come to learn.
Where you have taught, even the few, but two or three together, the divine has come to manifest.
Let your words raise in us noble thoughts.
Through your teaching, let harmony, beauty, and love be found in us.
As we observe your ways and the lives of those you've inspired, aid us in becoming more like God.

O holy Philosophers, your
   Words inspire us to seek,
And so through you, we raise ourselves
   To greater heights, without bleak
Opinions but true knowledge of
   Our ignorance. The beauty
Of wisdom enflames in us love,
   And through love, truth we do see.

And to the Divine-Workers we
  Give praise. You co-Creators
Who have walked the path we follow,
  Hear this our song. Your word spurs
Us to purity, your actions
  Show the will of the Seven-
Rayed Divinity. Look at us
  With joy on our ambition.

O great ones, mighty in wisdom, God-Working Bacchantes, we pray to you.

Great sages in whose paths we walk, you who seek after wisdom, and grasp the divine in love, hear us.

Most exalted Theurgists, keepers of the hieratic art, listen and be near.

In the heavens you have found your place, ruling the cosmos beside the Seven-Rayed King.

Each soul you see in its place, for you too have been there, before your divine ascent.

You direct the course of the world, the daimons of the Earth, with the authority of God.

Grant us wisdom after your ways, that, like you, we might descend into bodies perfectly and without attachment.

Set in our paths visions of the heavens so we might recognize our way home and join you in the eternal and
  sublime dance.

Let us know you that through your knowledge and wisdom we may better serve the divine.

The Evensong Prayers

O messengers from that realm which lies between lives, hear our prayer.

Great and sacred dead: ancestors, philosophers, and theurgists who have come before, we give you our praise.

Listen to our plea as the sun sets upon the day, you whose lives have also set, only to one day rise again in glory.

You have given life to the generations.

Your words have brought wisdom to the seeker.

Through your divine acts you have bestowed purity to those who live the mysteries.

By your presence we are made more like the divine image.

Let our lives be guided by your holy wisdom.

This we pray as we seek to engage in what is best for all humanity.

Readings for Lectio Divina

The Father mixed the spark of soul with two harmonious qualities, Intellect and divine Will, to which he added a third, pure Love, as the guide and holy bond of all things. – *Chaldean Oracles*, fr 44.3-5.

May I count him rich who is wise, and as for gold, may I possess so much of it as only a temperate man might bear and carry with him. – Plato, *Phaedrus*, 279c.

For the soul that descends for the salvation, purification, and perfection of this realm is immaculate in its descent. – Iamblichus, *De Anima*, VI.B.29.380.19-21.

But those souls that have been let go free, are unmixed, are entirely unmastered, are themselves of themselves, and are filled with the gods, are thereby also entirely freed from judgment. – Iamblichus, *De Anima*, VIII.A.44.546.12-17.

After the souls have been freed from generation… they administer the universe together with the gods… – Iamblichus, *De Anima*, VIII.B.53.458.6-7.

…and with souls, those that are pure reveal themselves as wholly removed from matter,… – Iamblichus, *De Mysteriis*, II.5.81.6-7.

PRAYER SERVICE FOR THE OBSERVATION OF HENE

Hour of Dew Prayer

Hail, final saviour, Lord of Daimons, hear our prayer!
Mighty King who knows the depths of our souls, we call to you.
Hearken, O Principality who turns us towards our proper place.
Now is the time that you, in the darkening of the moon, call all who love you.
Your hand opens the gate or closes it. Open it wide that we might know our spirit well.
Our words are now for you alone, that you do not keep us separate from our proper places.
At this time, show mercy upon us, that we may be perfected by your light.
Let our activities be pleasing through virtue, that we need not be corrected.
O Divine Governor of this darkling world, do not let us stumble in our blindness.

The Noontide Prayers and Hymns

We pray to you, O Image-Maker, master of daimons, protector of the sacred dead, hear us.
Upon the All-Receiver, Lord of this realm and the next, we call. Be with us.
O Purifier of Souls, reaper of all that is mortal, raise us unto you.
The pre-essential Demiurgos spoke, and in the wake of his words was you, governing the third realm.
Your words judge all deeds obscure and conspicuous.
Your judgment sets all souls in their proper place, even as we will one day be judged.
Through you let us leave this realm in peace and at the appropriate time.
In us, let your initiation always be a reminder of the divine work and the time we have to do it in this realm.
By your Name let those spirits which lead to purity guide us.

O holy Master of Daimons,
* Lord beneath the moon's bright sphere,*
We raise our voices in hymn to
* You. Through you we come to hear*
The voice of our daimon. Let us
* Hear the words of that mighty*
Spirit that it might guide us in
* The ways helpful to your See.*

Haides

And, O holy Creator, you
  Who were scattered that our souls
May be made perfect. Leader of
  The great theurgists, make our goals
Attainable in this realm and
  The next: the separation
Of principles to their correct
  Places, the Many made One.

Hear our prayer, O Scattered One who was broken upon primordial waters.
We call to you, O Lord of the Night who separates wholes into parts.
To you we speak praises, O Leader of the God-Working Bacchantes.
From your sub-lunar throne you oversee the separation of divine principles.
Where your rich wine spills from emptied cups, the divine workers rise in creative activities.
Where your frenzy overtakes the devout, nothing contrary to God remains.
Let your words inspire us towards the sacred rites.
Through your division let us see the hope of unity.
As we observe your holy ways, let our minds be united with Mind.

Great Master of Baccantes, we
  Sing to you, our Lord. Your rites
Bring forth all manner of good works
  And your Vision brings great sights.
Let your work separate all things
  Improper to their places,
Let your work correct all error
  In our lives through the ages.

O healer and saviour of souls,
  We hymn you with praise most high.
What has been scattered will be made

Whole through you, what is a lie
Is turned towards the Truth. Let us
See with your vision the Forms
Governing below and above
And so stay the coming storms.

O Lord and saviour of all the Earth, we pray to you.
Great healer who restores the divine reason principles so all is made whole and complete, hear us.
Most exalted image maker, who completes the divine plan in the realm of generation, listen and be near.
In the heavens you see the intelligible pattern written in light.
Each soul is given to you, for what has been rent you make whole, each proper to its series.
You direct the whole universe towards completion in the fullness of eternity.
Grant us salvation through your holy touch and panacea.
Set in our paths all which is within our series, that our orbits may carry us, in circular fashion, back to our
   beginnings.
Let us know you, for through you is all made complete.

The Evensong Prayers

O Divine Craftsman, Lord of daimons and generation, hear our prayer.
Great King who causes the odd to be separate from the even, opinion from knowledge, we give you our praise.
Listen to our plea, you great King, saviour, and maker of divine images.
You allow daimons to be known to those who are sown in their orbits.
Your will perfects souls.
Through your activity below we rise to our heights.
By your munificence, let us know ourselves through our daimons.
Let our lives be filled with all that is beneficial.
This we pray as we seek divine providence in the realm below.

Readings for Lectio Divina

Your sleep tears the soul free from the body's hold, whenever you undo nature's powerful bonds, bringing the long slumber, the endless one, to the living. – *Orphic Hymns*, 'To Death,' 3-5.

Then it is a fact that true philosophers make dying their profession, and that to them of all men death is least alarming. – Plato, *Phaedo*, 67e.

If I did not expect to enter the company, first, of other wise and good gods, and secondly of men now dead who are better than those who are in this world now, it is true that I should be wrong in not grieving at death. – Plato, *Phaedo*, 63b.

[I]f…the living and the dead arise out of each other and do this eternally, the soul will thus be eternal… – Iamblichus, *In Phaed*, fr. 3.6-7.

Daimon

PRAYER SERVICE FOR THE OBSERVATION OF HENE KAI NEA

Hour of Dew Prayer

Hail great daimon, ruler and guide of souls, hear our prayer!

Mighty Power, divine teacher and corrector of errors, we call to you.

Hearken, O guard and guide, be always at our sides.

Now is the time to come to us in our need, present in your terrible beauty.

Your purifying light leads us to divine order.

Our lives are corrected in your presence as we seek ever to rise to our proper height.

At this time, in the dark of the moon, we pray for your secret words to guide us.

Let our backs be straightened and our ways made worthy of divine reception.

O Power over mortal fate, help us to see providence's grace.

The Noontide Prayers and Hymns

We pray to you, our mighty daimons, governing spirits who guide our lives, hear us.

Upon the essential spirit set above each of us, leaders unto purity, we call: be with us.

O Spirits of Authority, guides and guardians of our souls, raise us unto you.

The duodecad set you above us, and you govern your wards according to divine decree.

Your words speak directly to our souls; we pray we may hear them as well.

Your series and orbit leads us to our places.

Through you, let us rise to become like God, so far as possible.

In us, set the divine spark ablaze that we may see the divine face which set us on our course.

By your Names, vouchsafed to us by the Master of Daimons, let us know you and be fulfilled.

To the spirit set over our
  Souls, we give praise. Hear our song
O mighty Authorities, great
  Guardians of our souls, long
Do we yearn for your presence in
  Our lives. To the one of twelve

Let us, through you, rise. May your Name
  Bring us the heavens to delve.

O daimons of our souls, hear this
  Hymn. You great, purifying
Spirits, leader of souls in their
  Orbits sown and adjoining,
Grant us your blessings and wisdom.
  Be to us a guardian
And guide, leading us to heaven's
  Swift orbit and brilliant Sun.

Hear our prayer, O guiding daimons overseeing our souls and lives.
We call to you, O leaders of souls who have not yet risen to angelic heights.
To you we speak praises, you holy, purifying spirits who stand above all mortal kind.
From above time you watch us, knowing everything about our souls, guide and guardian both.
Where your voices reach us, we transcend our lives to become more fully ourselves.
Where your activities are manifest, we become firmly bound to our lives.
Let your words come to us, guide us, and fulfil us, O mighty daimons!
Through your knowledge let us know all within our series.
As we observe your holy ways, let them be as beacons to us on the cyclical path.

O spirits: bright, governing, and
  Wise, we acclaim your glory!
You wonderful daimons who do
  Fill our lives: hear this, our plea
To your mercy and endless light.
  From generation's straightness
Lead us to the divine orbit
  Round heaven's strong aegis.

Keepers of souls, purifiers
  Most divine, in your care our
Souls do lie. Let your purity
  Awaken us in this hour
To the Mind of God. Guide us in
  Heavenly circuit, our wings
Regrown in the divine moment
  Between eternal callings.

O blessed Daimon, watcher and purifier of souls, we pray to you.
Great and holy spirit set above us by the divine Mind, hear us.
Most exalted guardian and guide, keeper of the souls in your care, listen and be near us.
In the heavens you steer our lives until the charioteer awakens.
Each soul in your keeping is guided by your all-seeing gaze.
You direct your ward with unceasing care until you are needed no more.
Grant us purity that our souls may awaken to divine illumination.
Set in our paths all that is necessary for us to regain control of our dual natures.
Let us know you that we may be better guided by your holiness.

The Evensong Prayers

O you Authorities over every person's soul, hear our prayer.
Great spirits, you who watch over us, guide us, and correct us, we give you our praise.
Listen to our plea, O wonderful daimons, guardians of this and each of our lives.
You lead us in our orbit, urging us to move in circular fashion.
Your activities bring our lives, even in our ignorance, into closer participation with what is better
  For all things: goodness and the Good.
Through your Names we come to know you, and so we invoke you that all may be fulfilled.
By your pre-eminent knowledge, O you who are set on high, direct our steps that we may have sure footing.
Let our lives align with the series of our soul.
This we pray as we seek your counsel this and every day.

Readings for Lectio Divina

Take careful council,
Know thyself,
Consult the daimon,
Undertake nothing without God. — *Delphic Maxim*

MONTHLY HIEROMENIAS

Monthly Hieromenias

FOR THE LAW WILL STATE THAT THERE ARE TWELVE FEASTS TO THE TWELVE GODS WHO GIVE THEIR NAMES TO THE SEVERAL TRIBES: TO EACH OF THESE THEY SHALL PERFORM MONTHLY SACRIFICES AND ASSIGN CHOIRS AND MUSICAL CONTESTS AND ALSO GYMNASTIC CONTESTS, AS IS SUITABLE BOTH TO THE GODS THEMSELVES AND TO THE SEVERAL SEASONS OF THE YEAR;.... FURTHER, THEY MUST DETERMINE, IN CONFORMITY WITH THE LAW, THE RITES PROPER TO THE NETHER GODS, AND HOW MANY OF THE CELESTIAL GODS SHOULD BE INVOKED AND WHAT OF THE RITES CONNECTED WITH THEM SHOULD NOT BE MINGLED BUT KEPT APART, AND PUT THEM IN THE TWELFTH MONTH, WHICH IS SACRED TO PLUTO....

PLATO, LAWS, VIII.828B-C

Laws Quotation for Months

Iamblichus

CHAPTER 7

Prayer Services for the Months

PRAYER SERVICE FOR THE MONTH OF PHYXIOSION

Celebrant:

Worshippers of the gods give ear. This is the hour for the Dew-time [or Noontide or Evensong] prayer. Let us invoke all the divinities and the holy Demiurgos, who reigns over them, with all our mind, and all our reason, and all our soul.[79]

All kneel on both knees, facing the same direction.[80] Everyone makes the gesture of invocation: arms raised and held outwards, with palms up.

All: O divine ones, be propitious.[81]

Raise one knee, touch the ground with the right hand.

All: O divine ones, be propitious.

Lift right hand, touch ground with the left hand.

All: O divine ones, be propitious.

Make full prostration: both knees, hands, and forehead touching the ground.

All: (three times) O Demiurgos, great king, be propitious.

---

[79] Alternatively: "with all our essence, our all power, and all our activity."
[80] Plethon does not specify a direction, or no such specification has survived to my knowledge. Use whichever direction is appropriate to your overall ritual praxis.
[81] Alternatively: "O gods, be propitious" or "O God, be propitious."

Helios

The Hour of Dew Prayer

We offer a prayer to the celestial Thunderer, at whose Word chaos flees.

Leader of the heavens, hear our call that our souls' orbits may come close to you.

Indestructible God, we have bowed before you in supplication.

You stood before the origins of all, and subdued the order of creation.

At your Word the sky was made stable and the soul given form, both eternal and temporal.

From the remains of chaos you had humanity created, and so we call upon you, O Saviour of all.

Beaming Lord, celestial sun and King of All, clear the path before us so we may walk in your ways.

By your Word, let the chaos of our origins be set in its place, that the better part of our souls may rule the worse.

Set your hand upon us, Lord of Freedom, and grant us the clear vision of our true home.

The Noontide Prayers and Hymns

Divine Word hear our prayer.

True One, Creator of Living Beings, hear our cry, you Protector of Wisdom.

Ruler of the heavens and Earth, Purifier of Souls, be propitious.

The pandemonium before creation raged and you silenced it.

The chaos before the rising of the sun cried out in rage, and you withstood it.

The bedlam of the darkly splendid world rose up, and the Truth of your Word subdued it.

Grant us Wisdom.

Speak to us Truth.

Prepare us so we may reach our goal.

O Hidden One, make yourself known.
Master of truth, speak your Word
And settle discordant daimons
Who shake when your voice is heard.
Celestial King of many
Names, Creative Mind, mighty
God, be near. Wielder of lightning
Who stood first before all were free.

Leader of Fate who changes the
  Course of time, you cast down those
Who would upset God's providence.
  Factious giants you dispose
So that creation may unfold.
  Great God, put to flight the storm
And set our feet upon the way
  So we may behold your form.

Holy Demiurgos, leader of divinities, holy Intellect, we pray to you.
Daimon of Daimons, Good God, Lord of Heaven, your names are without end
  And we call to you by all your names.
In the beginning, you raised your thunderbolt and slew the dragon.
The torrent of waters beat against you, but you placed them in their proper place.
Before the divine essences were set in their course, you stood above all.
There is none who may bar your way.
Open our eyes so we may behold you before setting foot upon the trail.
Protect us with your aegis that our souls may regain strength.
Each turn, before our lives begins, make us mighty in your wisdom.

Divine Council, hero-maker,
  Mind of God, and soul sower,
Voice who calls the divinities
  To order, Lightning-Thrower:
Hear us. Through your primordial
  Will the vast heavens shall be
Populated, and Earth, too. Set
  Our souls on the endless sea.

We set our lips to your praise, God,
  King of Heaven who purges

The ocean of its malcontent.
  Our souls stand on the verges
Of the heavens and sing to you.
  Sky-shaking power, please this hymn
Do hear upon your throne and look
  At us with favour not dim.

Hear this prayer, O great King of All, and be near us.
Lord of intellective flames who will move across the heavens, give ear.
Triumphant over the waters, your fire sets back the tides.
Glorying in the midday light, thoughts of darkness flee; through your blaze the heavens are made known to us.
To some are given the burnt offerings of the flesh, we offer you our thoughts.
Set your aureole upon our brows, O Lord.
Let the flames of our minds rise to you, O Demiurgos.
Let the flames rise to you and therein plant the seed of the flower of the mind.
Through its divine fragrance we will know you.

The Evensong Prayer

Chariot-driving Glory, eternal Sun, spoken Word, hear our prayer.
Great reflection of Eternity, our thoughts glorify your Names.
The song of the phoenix and pelican is yours.
In the darkness you sang that the words of your mind would take form.
For you rule the heavens and the earth, are lord of creation and destruction.
The Daughters of Night trail your path to the west.
In your dearth those who were asleep come to awaken.
In the stillness of night you rehearsed the heavens in their movements so providence may unfold.
As your image goes to harrow the foes of Truth, keep our souls always beneath your holy gaze.

Readings for Lectio Divina

This reality, then, that gives their truth to the objects of knowledge and the power of knowing to the knower, you must say is the idea of good, and you must conceive it as being the cause of knowledge, and of truth in so far as known. – Plato, *Republic*, 508e.

The leader of the celestial gods,… an intellect thinking himself, and turning his thoughts towards himself. – Iamblichus, *De Mysteriis*, VIII.3.263.1-4.

He has handed down the name of the god, which extends throughout the whole cosmos. – Iamblichus, *De Mysteriis*, VIII.5.268.2-3.

Law is said to be the "king of all." – *Letters*, 'To Agrippa, On Ruling,' fr 2.1.

For it exhorts its subjects toward noble practices, even as it apportions to each his proper worth. – *Letters*, 'To an Unknown Recipient, On Ruling,' fr 1.3-5.

Father of yourself, first creator, king who generates everything, supreme, who dominates on all – Plethon, *'All Year Hymn to Zeus.'*

PRAYER SERVICE FOR THE MONTH OF HÔRÊPHOROSION

The Hour of Dew Prayer

We offer a prayer to the Queen of the Earth, who brings the seasons each in their due time.

Leader of the four quarters of time, who is present at sowing, reaping, and threshing, hear our call that our souls' orbits may come close to you.

Dark veiled Lady, we have bowed before you in supplication.

You stood in the Field of the Blessed and enabled souls to rise up to their new lives.

At your direction flowers will bloom or whither, and so too all life, and so we call upon you, O All-Nourishing Lady.

From the remains of one season you cause the next to arise, the power of movement is yours to bestow.

Charming Lady, Queen over the movement of life, grant us the power to proceed after return, return after proceeding, and remain after returning.

By your stillness before all beginnings are all activities measured, let each season of our soul be imbued with the perfection of movement.

Set your hand upon us, Lady of Life and Growth, and grant us the pure, circular movement of all divine beings.

The Noontide Prayers and Hymns

Divine Throne, hear our prayer.

True basis of all seasons, who Sends Forth Gifts, hear our cry, you Protector of Life.

Ruler who Brings Forth Movement, Great Mother, be propitious.

The movement of all souls relies upon you, without you there is no procession.

The wisdom of your series halts all motion, or brings it forth.

The silenced chaos remains still, except for your Word.

Grant us abiding.

Speak to us of procession.

Prepare us so we may return.

Demeter

O holy Lady of first shoots,
  Life's giver and Movement's Queen
Great Mother please hear this, our prayer.
  You have silenced chaos' dream
And given movement to what was
  Once still. Procession, without
You, is impossible, for you
  Are the source of every sprout.

We sing to you hymns of holy
  Time, O Queen of Life. Listen
To our song and be near, Mistress
  Of the golden sword. Let none
Pass who do not enter into
  Procession, but for now let
Us abide with you, O Mother,
  Our home let us not forget.

Holy Mother, great Keeper of Time, we pray to you.
Daimon of Heavenly Orbits, Queen who lights the way, your names are ten-thousand fold.
In the beginning you raised the golden sword and flaming brand and the banished chaos held still.
The torrent of unlawfulness halted at your demand, lest all motion be starved from the world.
Before the seasons can pass, your permission must be granted.
There is none who may advance without your say.
Open the way before us, do not let us starve, abandoned, when it is our time to proceed from our allotted place.
Protect us from lawlessness, let our steps be in line with Providence.
Each turn, as we strive to circle the heavens, make us sure in our stride.

Bringer of the Law, let us now
  Abide with you so we may
Know the ways of Providence's

Creed that we not may gainsay
Heaven's law. As our orbits pause
   In your presence, inspire us
With your blessings. Brace our resolve
   And fill us with your chalice.

Bringer of Seasons, Wholesome Queen
   Of All, to you we pray. Grant
Us fulfilment in your presence
   And do not let us recant
The sacred truths and rites. Giver
   Of motion and life, set our
Course, the Helmsman's way, and grant us
   A time where life is not dour.

Hear this prayer, O great Queen and Leader, and be near us.
Lady of intelligible time, measure of procession, give ear.
Triumphant over the seasons, who gives forth life, your justice halts all in their place or brings them movement
   again.
Glorying as we abide in oneness, you bring forth thoughts of procession; through you all movement is known to us.
To some are given the power of self-motion, even they rely upon you.
Set your torch before us, light our way, O Queen.
Let the movement of our chariots be pleasing to you.
Let the movement guided by the helmsman who sees your light be sure.
Through you we will find our way.

The Evensong Prayer

Chariot-driving Glory with dragons yoked to your will, eternal motion before motion, hear our prayer.
Great Queen of All, our orbits glorify your names.
The songs of all the seasons are yours, without you there is no life.

In your absence, all that remains is darkness, without movement there is no life.
For you rule remaining, proceeding, and returning.
The yield which is your due is all green life and orbiting souls.
In your still motion all things become possible.
In the wake of your wide orbit, all may circle the heavens.
As you seek the birth of life in the afterlife, let your flame keep our souls safe upon their trails.

Readings for Lectio Divina

You are growth and blooming,… - Orphic Hymns, *'To Eleusinian Demeter,'* 10.

And why all this longing for propagation? Because this is the one deathless and eternal element in our mortality. – Plato, *Symposium*, 206e.

For she, first in power, receives the birth of all these in her inexpressible womb… – *Chaldean Oracles*, fr. 56.4-5.

It is the Mistress of Life and possesses full measures of the many wombs. – *Chaldean Oracles*, fr. 96.2-3.

[T]he immaterial cause that pervades the earth, which sustains bodies with life… – Iamblichus, *In Tim*, fr. 20.4-5.

The 'sowing' of souls into vehicles [is] the first birth. – Iamblichus, *In Tim*, fr. 85.6-7.

Apollon

PRAYER SERVICE FOR THE MONTH OF OULIOSION

The Hour of Dew Prayer

We offer a prayer to the Lord of Health and Harmony, whose flaming darts ward off all evil.

Leader of the Muses, harmonious Lutenist, hear our call that our souls' orbits may come close to you.

Succouring Lord, we have bowed before you in supplication.

You stood in the heavens and balanced the poles, infusing harmony into all humanity.

At your bidding the seasons of earth and soul became equal.

From the remains of the day you bring about evening, from evening, day, and so we call upon you, O foreseeing Lord.

Averter of Evil, driving the sun around its course, mark us with your blessings as we rise up to proceed through the divine journey.

By your holy song make the way clear to us, that we do not become lost upon the road.

Set your hand upon us, Rescuing Lord, and grant us true knowledge of what lies before us.

The Noontide Prayers and Hymns

Divine and radiant King, hear our prayer.

True Light of the Eastern sky, hear our cry, O foe of evil.

Ruler of the heavens, protector of harmonious souls, be propitious.

The dissonance before the first string is plucked is dispelled at your song.

The discord of the stranded chariot wreaked its havoc, and you calmed souls in distress.

The cacophony of the serpent is overcome, the might of your vision destroyed it.

Grant us harmony.

Speak to us of perfection.

Prepare us so we may regain the health of a sacred life.

Great Father of harmonious
  Light, giver of health, we sing
To you praises of joy. For you
  Took your bow and set to spring

Golden rays down on evil's head.
  And you rout out disquiet
In heart and soul. Sound of Health, grant
  Us a place at your banquet.

Lord of the Two Heavens, beaming
  King of light and health, all in
Your series brings life to the soul.
  Your oracles calm the din
And your inspiration opens
  Our minds. Great Lord of peaceful
Melodies, grant us respite from
  Discord and wicked evil.

Holy King, father of health and healing, we pray to you.
Daimon of harmony, sound of health, Lord of Heaven, we call to you by your names.
In the beginning you illuminated all the greater kind so they might move in one accord.
The torrent of burning smoke strove against your song, but you overcame and set all in harmony.
Before we may be at peace in our orbits, your word brought peace into being.
There is none who may cause illness or harm in your presence.
Open our eyes that we might know our place in Providence.
Protect us with your song, that discord may not reach our ears.
Each turn and orbit of our lives, let them be melodious, one perfect note in a sea of divine symphony.

Great radiant Father of the
  Heavens, hear our prayer. King
Of harmony, looser of darts
  Upon evil's head, we sing
To you our praise. Illuminate
  Our minds and open our souls,

Set us in line with divine ways,
Let us pass ungodly tolls.

Illness' foe and bestower of
Harmony, radiant King,
Shine upon all in their orbits
And our soul: let them take wing.
Lord of light and balance, father
Of healing and sacred muse
Open our eyes and fill our hearts
That our minds may be set loose.

Hear this prayer, O great King of Heaven, and be near us.
Lord of heavenly light, leader of inspiration, give ear.
Triumphant over discord and darkness, Lord of Harmony, your beams pierce the darkness and bring forth light.
Glorying in victory over the cacophony of sibilant dissonance, your song brings peace to even the most unruly of steeds.
To some are given the harshness of conflicting life, you bring about oneness in body and soul.
Setting down your bow and sword, your enemies conquered, you play the harmony of the spheres.
Let the light of your glory pierce the darkness which mires our souls' chariots.
Let the light harmonize our lives and souls.
Through your song let the charioteer bring peace to his steeds.

The Evensong Prayer

Chariot-Lord driven by winged steeds so noble, bright one, slayer of evil and bringer of Harmony, hear our prayers.
Great King of Heaven who sails over the sea of clouds, our orbits glorify your names.
The songs of your lips bring sweetness to all souls, O King of Day and Night.
Into the darkness you journey, but you forever conquer and rise again.
For you rule all that is brilliant, O sun of Intellect.

The night of the soul is overcome through you as your song brings us rest.
In your stillness all souls orbit you through the heavens, let ours not be lost to the night.
In the spreading darkness, be our hope.
As you purify all upon your path, in this realm and the next, let your rays touch us with their glory.

Readings for Lectio Divina

You have infused harmony into the lot of all men, giving them an equal measure of winter and summer. – Orphic Hymns, *'To Apollon,'* 20-1.

[A]nd having first attained to self-mastery and beautiful order within himself… – Plato, *Republic,* 443d.

Virtue, then, as it seems, would be a kind of health and beauty and good condition of the soul… – Plato, *Republic,* 444e.

Priding himself on the harmony of light… – *Chaldean Oracles,* 71.1.

[T]he beauty of self-control extends throughout all the virtues, and harmonizes all the virtues into one accord, and instils into them symmetry and blending with one another. – Iamblichus, *Letters,* 'To Arete, on Self-Control,' III fr. 6.2-4.

Dionysus in Zeus, for instance, Asklepios in Apollo, the Charites in Aphrodite. – Sallustius, *Concerning the Gods and the Universe,* VI.

PRAYER SERVICE FOR THE MONTH OF ESCHARAION

The Hour of Dew Prayer

We offer a prayer to She who is Home to all divinities.

Leader of initiates, hear our call that our souls' orbits may come close to you.

Buttressing Goddess, we have bowed before you in supplication.

You stood at the centre of the high dwelling and gave life to all.

At your will all are given home and comfort.

From the remains of the embers of your life-giving activity all souls are sent forth, and so we call upon you, O most favoured divinity.

Honourable Lady, hearth and source of life, let our place remain even as we step away from our heavenly home.

By your purity make our place fixed and stable.

Set your hand upon us, Granter of Unwithering Youth, and give us sacred initiation into the never-ending orbit of the initiates.

The Noontide Prayers and Hymns

Divine Hearth, hear our prayer.

True guardian of abiding souls, hear our cry, O you who brings us closer to the source of all.

Ruler of purity and the eternal abode, be propitious.

The security of all souls at rest lies in you.

The basis of the heavens lies at your feet.

The divine abode is protected on all sides by your purity.

Grant us safety.

Speak to us of foundations.

Prepare us so we may be secure whether home or abroad.

Great Queen, divine foundation and
  Home, we praise you with this song
And sacred hymn. Great Mother who
  Secures us the whole night long
Until we are ready to set
  Forth by day. In the centre

Hestia

You give refuge to all within
  The safety of your harbour.

Sacred Hearth, purity's Mother,
  Who secures virtue for those
In your embrace, hear us! Great Guard
  On four corners, you who knows
The ways of hearth and home, let your
  Blessings rain like holy oil
Upon us. Keeper of divine
  Homes from every needless toil.

Holy Queen, mother of safeguarding purity, we pray to you.
Daimon of the divine home, dripping with holy oil, your names call us to remain with our series.
In the beginning you secured the hearth so souls might have a home in the heavens.
The torrent of sweet-smelling incense causes all to remember you and give homage to your blessings.
Before the heavens were set upon their foundation you stood at their centre.
There is none who may cause harm to any within your presence.
Open the portcullis that we may return or proceed in safety.
Protect us from all that may endanger our journey.
Each turn, as we rise to our place, make us secure in our orbits.

Sacred Queen, spirit of virtue,
  You who secure the ceaseless
Abode of all divinities,
  Hear our prayer. You, great basis
Of all refuges, standing at
  Heaven's centre, close the gate
And guard all those within your care
  And those in your home who wait.

For *after you our journey must*
  Begin, so let us achieve
Victory over pollution
  And do not let us bereave
Leaving your abode. Sheltering
  Lady and Guard, let your depth
Fill us and your ramparts protect
  Us as we pursue your breadth.

Hear this prayer, O great Queen and Guardian, and be near us.
Lady of heavenly refuge, you who are inviolate, give ear.
Triumphant over impurity, who protects all within her care, your bulwarks give comfort to souls.
Glorying in your purity, you set the foundation of the eternal realm in order.
To some are given the inequities of an unvirtuous life, you give shelter to the virtuous.
Set your hearth before us that we may shelter in its warmth and protection.
Let the heavenly ramparts protect our souls.
Let the heavenly light purify the path from you and back.
Through your comfort, let us be safe in our foundations.

The Evensong Prayer

Chariot-bereft Queen who forgoes travel to guard all from the centre, hear our prayers.
Great source of purity, our orbits glorify your names.
The songs in praise of you stem from the foundations of the heavens, O Queen of Sheltering Warmth.
In your presence, no impurity may accrete upon the vehicle of the soul.
For you rule over all who protect their realms, and offer respite to all guardians.
The foundation built upon you shall forever remain sacrosanct, even in the darkest of nights.
In your stillness keep vigil over the essences of our souls.
In the dark warmth of the earthen hearth, let our lives flourish.
As you remain ever pure, let us be purified.

Readings for Lectio Divina

May you raise the holy initiates in these sacred rites, may you grant them unwithering youth, wealth as well, prudence and purity. – *Orphic Hymns*, 'To Hestia,' 3-4.

Home of the blessed gods, men's mighty buttress, eternal, many-shaped, beloved… – *Orphic Hymns*, 'To Hestia,' 6.

It is necessary to propose the virtues which, from creation, purify and lead back to God: Faith, Truth, and Love. – *Chaldean Oracles*, fr. 6.1-2.

For the purification of our luminous body there is a need to get rid of material defilements… – *Chaldean Oracles*, fr. 119.1-2.

[I]t is purification from passions and freedom from the toils of generation and unification with the divine first principle that the ascent through invocations procures for the priests… - Iamblichus, *De Mysteriis*, I.12.41.13-15.

So it is through an intellect that is pure and free from all bodily influences to mould it that the vision of virtue comes about. – Iamblichus, *Letters*, 'To Sopater, on Virtue,' XVI, fr. 2.1-2.

Poseidon

PRAYER SERVICE FOR THE MONTH OF ENNOSIGAIOSION

The Hour of Dew Prayer

Most holy King, Earth Shaker, who brings forth new life, listen to our prayer.

Great Holder of the Earth, whose drink regenerates all vitality, heed us.

O divine Nurturer of Life, host of the feast of immortality, be near us.

From you flows the starry way towards generation.

Your daughters accompany all along the proceeding path.

For they are the triple triad and you their monad, the source of their completion.

You who are the Tamer of Horses, our steed is unruly: lend us your aid.

You who tame the flowing way, may we proceed beneath your shield.

You whose drink gives renewed life, let us sip from your golden cup.

The Noontide Prayers and Hymns

Divine Watcher, Host of Feasts, hear our prayer.

True Securer of Safe Passage, hear our cry, O shaker of the sea.

Ruler of the wide sea of descent, guide to the lost, be propitious.

The sound of your song reveals true paths to those who would traverse the starry sea into generation.

The silvery hue of your tokens bring hope to all who see them.

The waves calm and the way is made clear when they are brought forth.

Grant us safety on our voyage.

Speak sweet songs of distant places that we might know them and not falter.

Prepare us that we may know the way to proceed.

We raise our voices to the great
    King of Feasts and earth-shaker,
The most holy Lord moves us
    In procession and does spur
Us around our orbits. Watcher
    Of the world, who smoothes the path

Before us, we give praise to you
  And ask to be spared from wrath.

Sing your song that we may know the
  Way by your honey'd words and
Let us navigate the starry
  Heavens until we find land.
Raise your strong hand and subdue the
  Cold waves of desolation
And open the way before us
  So our passage may be won.

Holy Father, whose passage thunders like a herd of mighty steeds, we pray to you.
Daimon of safe passage, Lord of the Starry Sea, we call you by your many names.
In the beginning you raised the land in the midst of the seas so living beings could inhabit generation and number
    the same as in the heavens.
The torrent of icy waves threatened to drown the world, but you raised your trident and stilled them.
Before souls could proceed from their heavenly circuit, you made the way ready, the mind willing in divine
    obedience and wisdom.
There is none who can bar passage into generation once you have granted it.
Open the gates between the worlds so we may pass in safety.
Protect us with your coat and armour and mighty sword that we may be protected with triple-barbed strength.
Each turn will teach us more of our souls, but only if you allow us to proceed.

Holy Father, who guides vessels
  So they may safely proceed
Around their orbit, bless us. King
  And holy spirit, we heed
Your song and journey towards the
  Gate you've opened for each soul

Which leaves the harbour's safety to
  Sail forth and reach heaven's goal.

Make welcome to us your holy
  Realm as we descend into
Generation to find what is
  Proper to our souls in lieu
Of a life unexamined. Let
  The mists of your home refresh
Us on our voyage. Help us, King,
  As we seek to put on flesh.

Hear this prayer, O great King of Hospitality, and be near us.
Lord of heavenly descent, advisor to kings and gods, give ear.
Triumphant over foes, splintering barriers in twain, Lord of Earth and Starry sea, your golden chariot stills the
    way before all.
Glorying in your kingdoms, you provide hospitality to all the greater kinds and fortify them for their journeys.
To some are given the hardship and misplaced touchstones, you make the course clear and the way calm.
Setting down your trident and sword, the path between worlds opens at your command.
Let the waves not crush us.
Let the mist rejuvenate us.
Through your generosity may our chariots travel the course as though you were at the reins.

The Evensong Prayer

Chariot-commanding King, who travels over smooth waves and fresh-hewn land, hear our prayers.
Great giver of divine gifts that allow souls to make their way, our orbits glorify your names.
The song guides all those who may be lost and encourages all who proceed towards generation.
Into the darkness of the depths you have sailed, and as you proceed your spray cleanses and perfects all upon
    whom it rains.
For you rule the procession from above to below and the way is calm at your word.

The light of your cloak illumines the way forward as you bid us victory and blessings.
In your stillness make for us the waves, the passage clear.
In the happiness of your lands let us know a joy to fortify us in our orbits.
As you give us the pure steeds which guide us, give us the wisdom to direct them.

Readings for Lectio Divina

Deep-roaring ruler of the waters, the waves are your blossoms… – *Orphic Hymns*, 'To Poseidon,' 4-5.

Therefore, all things are obliged to remain forever in ceaseless motion… – *Chaldean Oracles*, fr. 12.4-5.

But the soul that tends downwards drags in its train signs of chains and punishments… – Iamblichus, *De Mysteriis,* II.7.84.11-12.

[E]very procession of illuminating light, proceeding from the Father, whilst visiting us as a gift of goodness, restores us again gradually as a unifying power, and turns us to the oneness of our conducting Father, and to a deifying simplicity. – Dionysius the Areopagite, *'On the Heavenly Hierarchy,'* I.1.120B.

PRAYER SERVICE FOR THE MONTH OF ANTHEIAION

The Hour of Dew Prayer

Divine and most holy Queen, Mother of Rain and Queen of the Sojourning Barque, listen to our prayer.

Great Lady of Heaven, whose Word gives life, heed us.

O divine Deathless Saviour, Whose Hand is Above us, life does not exist without you, be near us.

From you blows the wind which moves the Helmsman's ship.

Your soft breezes nourish souls as they sail along the descending way.

For your cooling gales nourish life.

You who are the Queen of the Chariot, guide our charioteers along their course.

You who cause flowers to grow, nourish our souls with the same care.

You whose names outnumber the stars in the sky, let one be spoken for us.

The Noontide Prayers and Hymns

Divine Mother, Queen of Heaven, hear our prayer.

True source of life in generation, radiant light, hear our cry

O you who speaks the life-giving words.

Ruler of life-springing love, who rides the beasts outward, be propitious.

The command of your Word causes us to go forth before you, full of life.

The breeze you send to mortals invigorates us.

The blessings of new life and youth are borne from you.

Grant us movement.

Speak to us of procession.

Prepare us that we safely traverse the chasm between here and our celestial abodes.

A song of praise we raise to you
*   O Mother, heavenly Queen,*
Life's Source, Lady of cool breezes,
*   Be near us. Host of the green*
Pastures and the flowered meadows,
*   All who proceed are in debt*
To you, for your series sends forth
*   All to the world without threat.*

Hera

Let your peaceful winds and rains fall
  Upon the paths of heaven
That the sweet aroma of your
  Blessings may rise as we run
Along our orbits' ways. Giver
  Of life, Queen of bright plumage,
Who gives life to every soul and
  We pray to your lineage.

Holy Mother, Mother of Wind and Rain, we pray to you.
Daimon of life-nourishing union, Lady of Heaven, your names give sustenance to all who hear them.
In the beginning you animated the souls coming from the mixing bowl so they might spring forth to their orbits.
The torrent of winds and storms you overcame, and the sphinx is set upon all who would threaten what you hold.
Before life may proceed into generation, you speak it into motion.
There is none who may remain still in the face of your life-provoking wind.
Open the womb of the heavens that we may race with our celestial steeds.
Protect us from stumbling folly and hubris that our journey be smooth.
Each turn in our orbit brings us to you; allow us, through you, to advance.

O Queen of Heaven, who sweeps souls
  Into the cosmos on light
Winds, be propitious. You provoke
  Souls to move along their bright
Trails and discipline hubris' vain
  Champions. All move forward
At your command, rushing towards
  The world when your voice is heard.

So grant us motion and spur us
  To life-sustaining unions
With like souls through intellective

Love and bless us through the sun's
Enlivening activity.
   Your virtue guides us around
Our orbits' paths and directs us
   To where our ends may be found.

Hear this prayer, O great Queen of life-promoting unions, and be near us.
Lady of Heaven and Earth, who inspires all to move forward, give ear.
Triumphant over envy, Queen of Life, your storms buffet those who cling to ways that should be abandoned.
Glorying in your virtue, you put aright all those who wildly roam away from their series.
To some are given confusion and discordant movement, you guide souls in the proper direction.
Setting your joyousness in every life, your tokens send forth the vehicle of the soul.
Let the gentle winds of your blessings direct us.
Let the gentle rains of your blessings nourish us.
Through your many names let us be borne gently around our paths.

The Evensong Prayer

Chariot-encouraging Queen, who travels with hawks and cranes, hear our prayers.
Great source of life on Earth, our orbits glorify your names.
The songs of rain and wind and the constellations direct us on the right path, O Queen of Refreshing Breezes.
In the face of glory the generations of noble souls have proceeded upon their needful course.
For you rule all who no longer remain still and would now come to life.
The rainbow path accompanies you, your nourishing rains give it life.
In your stillness life grows in darkness and spills forth into generation, let our lives be joyous beneath your hand.
In the voyage of our life, let our goals come to our hands and, like the sacred Fleece, grant us divine rulership over
   our proper domain.
As you send us forth let your blessings rain upon us.

Readings for Lectio Divina

The soft breezes you send to mortals nourish the soul... – *Orphic Hymns*, 'To Hera,' 2.

Thus when it is perfect and winged it journeys on high and controls the whole world, but one that has shed its wings sinks down until it can fasten on something solid, and settling there it takes to itself an earthly body which seems by reason of the soul's power to move itself. – Plato, *Phaedrus*, 246b.

Receiving in her womb the processions from the intelligibles... and she sends forth the channels of corporeal life and contains within herself the centre of the procession of all beings. – *Chaldean Oracles*, fr. 189.

[B]ut the individual spirit vehicles proceeding and being given shape in accord with the life-principles of the encosmic gods. – Iamblichus, *In Tim*, fr. 84.7-8

Aphrodite

PRAYER SERVICE FOR THE MONTH OF PHILOMEIDÊSION

The Hour of Dew Prayer

Most holy Lady of the Fair Voyage, who brings beauty to the chariot of the soul, listen to our prayer.

Great Luminous One, whose light illuminates all souls with your rays, heed us.

O divine Diverter of Unlawful desires, you who harmonizes between separation and creation, be near us.

From you comes mighty Necessity, which brings all souls into generation.

Your children seek to raise all souls to the heights, but first we must journey down into the splendidly beautiful world.

For you allow those who participate you to proceed in joy, not inclining too far in any direction.

You who are the Harmony between opposites, by your hand help us control the uncontrollable steed.

You who cause generation to shine with intellective beauty, let us follow that beauty as we descend and ascend once more.

You whose form is reflected in all creation, let us proceed beneath the glory of your wing.

The Noontide Prayers and Hymns

Divine Mother of Love, who fills the sanctuary with joy, hear our prayer.

True begetter of harmony through friendship, who raises all through beauty and lawful desire,

Hear our cry, you Queen of Harmonious Forms.

Ruler of symphony-inclining words, Heaven-Born, be propitious.

The song of your lips raises a passion for peace in all who hear it.

The scions of your series guide us towards generation that we might once again ascend to you.

The caress of your hand reconciles every discordant note.

Grant us the beatific vision to fortify us.

Speak to us of the love of friendship, which brings justice and raises souls.

Prepare us that we may carry out our roles in a disharmonious world.

Love's Queen and Mother, we sing to
*   You. Harmonious Lady*
Of unions, hear our song. You were

160

Born of the heavens' decree
And raise all who praise you to a
   Vision of Beauty. Your acts
Bring life into the cosmos
   And kindred souls it attracts.

Raise us in your love, O Lady
   And Queen, that we may produce
Intellective unions, divine
   Concordances, and transduce
The lower to the higher. O
   Love's Queen, you House of Delight,
Place within us the desire for
   Love and set us on our flight.

Holy Queen and Consort, you whose passage reconciles all opposites in its wake, we pray to you.
Daimon of the Form of Beauty, Lady of the House of Jubilation, your names give sustenance to all who hear
   them.
In the beginning you gave birth to love and its harbingers so all might find harmony in their souls.
The torrent of ocean foam and heavenly stars you surpassed that your beauty could be a beacon for all travellers.
Before souls proceed from their home, you instil in them the desire for your union that they might seek the higher
   from this world of shadowy images.
There is none who can resist your call, which brings equilibrium to the reason-principles in all things.
Open the barriers which brought strife into our lives that we may pass them by safely.
Protect us from not recognizing the beauty in every person's life.
Each turn in our orbit shall remind us of the beauty you have set in the worlds above and below.

O Consort of Creation, Great
   Queen, Heaven's delight and grace,
   Set in balance love's desire and
   Set for us our journey's pace

That we may quickly return to
  Union with our orbit's Light
With our eyes opened to see your
  Indwelling gift with true sight.

Great Mother and harmonizer
  Of polarity, conquer
Once again discord's image and
  Bring joy to those who alter
Inharmonious ways with love.
  Set within us true Beauty
With dove's eyes gazing through matter's
  Dross, your Love do let us see.

Hear this prayer, O great Queen of harmony-procuring love, and be near us.
Lady of Grace, who causes joyous unions between enemies, give ear.
Triumphant over Discord, who brings joy to all the people, your actions bring all to fulfilling happiness.
Glorying in your beauty, you reconcile above with below in pursuit of the One.
To some are given the rewards of physical allure, your true nature transcends the body, let those with eyes see!
Setting your mantle aside, you show the faithful your true, invisible form, O Queen of the Form of Beauty.
Let us not mistake outer beauty for inner harmony.
Let all the world of generation lead us upwards to you.
Through your love, let us strive for perfection in this life and the next.

The Evensong Prayer

Chariot-compelling Queen, whose doves and falcons cry at your approach, hear our prayers.
Great bestower of concord, Queen of the Morning Star, our orbits glorify your names.
The song of your presence balances untamed passions, O Richly Crowned Daughter of the Creator.
In secret you enter the heart and lie with unblemished souls, bringing them to divine rapture.
For you rule over the apple and the heart, the body and the mind.

The Lords of Love and Ladies of Harmony attend your every gesture, their presence bespeaks of your pleasure.
In your stillness the quiet moment of realization is achieved in us, we ready ourselves to begin the upward journey home.
In the heat of passionate desire, let our actions bring beauty into the world.
As you remain in the heavens, be also in our hearts and before our eyes.

Readings for Lectio Divina

[Y]ou have yoked the world, you control all three realms… - *Orphic Hymns*, 'To Aphrodite,' 4-5.

Therefore, boast of the harmony under which the mortal body exists. – *Chaldean Oracles*, fr. 97.3.

It is not that the body and soul interact with one another or with the tones, but since the inspiration of the gods is not separated from the divine harmony,… it is shared by it in suitable measures. – Iamblichus, *De Mysteriis*, III.9.119.7-11.

If we say that, in the universe, being as it is one single living being, possessing a common life in all parts of itself, the communion of like powers, or the conflict of contrary ones, or a certain affinity of the active for the passive principle propels together like and suitable elements, pervading in virtue of a single sympathy even the most distant things as if they were most contiguous, there is stated in this way something of the truth and of the necessary consequences of sacrifices… – Iamblichus, *De Mysteriis*. V.7.207.8-208.1.

PRAYER SERVICE FOR THE MONTH OF SÔTEIRAION

The Hour of Dew Prayer

Most holy Lady, Protectress and Saviour, listen to our prayer.

Great Lady of Courage in Battle, who guards the way from above to below, heed us.

O divine Foresight and Counsellor, who offers souls respite from evil, be near us.

From you is the source of wisdom, by which all may plot a safe course.

Your realm holds the stuff of the chariots which all divinities ride.

For you bring safety and Prudence to the virtuous.

You who are the one who pours the libations of victory, let us be victorious over the trials of generation.

You who lie concealed in a garment of mystery and intelligible armour, make us invulnerable to unvirtuous temptation.

You whose spear and bow destroy evil, give us a full measure of peace as we return to the source of all.

The Noontide Prayers and Hymns

Divine Warrior and Maiden, Defender of Wisdom, Saviour of Souls, hear our prayer.

True guardian and protectress, hear our cry O sacred Counsellor.

Ruler of the fiery aether, healer and giver of hospitality, be propitious.

The cry of your voice overcomes the din of calamity and war.

The exercise of your skill brings salvation to all virtuous people.

The look of your eyes causes even the impetuous to become prudent.

Grant us health and wisdom to see us through our journey.

Speak to us of plans and strategies that we may not be overcome.

Prepare us that we may conquer all which stands in the way, both within and without.

O Divine Maiden with eyes of
  Mist, Saviour and Guard, we pray
To you. Skilled in arms and council
  You protect all souls and slay
Within us unvirtuous wants.
  Your flashing eyes warn even
The most impudent and sets them
  Aright, your battle hard-won.

Athena

Saviour and Immaculate Queen,
Who foresees trouble and snuffs
It at its root, do not let us
Go astray, you who rebuffs
All who move against the divine Mind. None can resist the blade
Of your sharp wisdom, and againstyour bright shield evil is stayed.

Holy Queen of Victory, you who cleanse the mind of impurities, we pray to you.
Daimon of Foresight and inspired frenzy, your names give sustenance to all who hear them.
In the beginning you came from the Mind of the Father, and you distribute wisdom to all the starry sky.
The torrent of unbridled passion was overcome by you, for you saw passion and anger subdued by reason.
Before the face of chaos you gave wise counsel leading to victory and the setting into order all the stars of the
heavens.
There is none who stands against you when you raise your aegis and spear.
Open the chariot way to us in our journey into generation.
Protect us from all harm as we end this season of Procession.
Each turn in our orbit raises in us wisdom and foresight, through you, that we, too, may serve as faithful
guardians to those who come after.

Heavenly warrior, protect
Those on procession's path and
Raise your aegis against evil
As it rises in the hand
Of darkness and ignorance. Set
Your wisdom on high and guard
Us as we ascend from this life
So that our souls are not marred.

Great Queen, who has the Creator's
Ear, Pure Lady, Defender
Of Virtue, bring us sweetly to

An end that is not bitter
From defeat. Mother of Prudence
Upturn the wrong, give foresight
To the virtuous, and strength to
Those all whom evil does fight.

Hear this prayer, O great Queen who gives counsel even unto the Celestial Creator, and be near us.
Lady of Good Health and Purity, who brings victory against adversity, give ear.
Triumphant over imprudence, mighty Maiden and inventive Queen, your actions bring all to fulfilling happiness.

Glorying in your prudence, you inspire others to virtuous lives.
To some are given honesty and wise action, your hand is set over those who act with foresight.
Setting sight upon the enemies of righteous souls, you stand to conquer all who seek to overturn the right with
wrong.
Let the words of your counsel guide our course.
Let the shield of wisdom protect us from our own folly.
Through your skill and ingenuity let us have safe passage as we come close to the end of our outward-moving
journey.

The Evensong Prayer

Chariot-guiding Warrior, who leads the divine steeds in their charge, hear our prayers.
Great Lady of Chastity and Virtue, our orbits glorify your names.
The song of battle rings out from your lips, O holy Trumpet of War and Saviour of heaven and earth.
In times of trouble you rain your glory down from star-swept heights.
For you rule the battle-cry and the wisdom of its use.
The song of triumph is yours as you vanquish impudence and iniquity from the heavens and souls.
In your stillness let us see the mind of the Father from which you sprang.
In the frenzy of battle, give us clarity to know what is right and to protect those who cannot protect themselves.
As you guard us at the end of our Procession, give us foreknowledge of what awaits our return.

Readings for Lectio Divina

[Y]ou bring madness to the wicked, you bring prudence to the virtuous… – *Orphic Hymns*, 'To Athene,' 9.

For it is not by ignorance but by knowledge that men counsel well. – Plato, *Republic*, IV.428b

There is no way, after all, that those who turn aside the assaults of the world of nature and generation can achieve this through the employment of passions. – Iamblichus, *De Mysteriis*, I.13.44.2-4.

He explains the 'war' as that faculty which utterly destroys the unordered and irregular and material nature, and the 'wisdom' as immaterial and transcendent intellection… – Iamblichus, *In Tim*, fr 21.4-6.

This, then, receives its existence principally from the pure and perfect intellect. – Iamblichus, *Letters*, 'To Asphalius, On Wisdom,' Letter IV, fr. 1.4-5.

Hephaestus

PRAYER SERVICE FOR THE MONTH OF POLYPHRÔNION

The Hour of Dew Prayer

Most holy Lord, Renowned of Skill, listen to our prayer.

Great and Ingenious King, whose resourcefulness fortifies all those who voyage home, heed us.

O divine Craftsman, who engraves godly thoughts in every soul, be near us.

From you comes the shape of all the arts, through these mortals see the light of heaven.

Your hand forges the thunderbolts of the mind which the sages grasp with hoary hands.

For you know the proportions of all created things.

You who tame all things in generation, and puts them in their place, help us to stand at your right side in governance.

You who govern the architecture of creation, guide us now as a master builder.

You whose name imbues creation with excellence, so imbue our souls as we return to our soulful duties.

The Noontide Prayers and Hymns

Divine Architect and Chief of Builders, hear our prayer.

True crafter from divine fire, hear our cry, O fashioner of beautiful souls.

Ruler of all the arts, divine armourer, Lord of Order, be propitious.

The spear from your hand always aims true, with it justice is restored.

The heavens rejected you, but you rose again from the depths and were established in your craft.

The might of your hammer shapes the world around you.

Grant us the skill to govern by the side of you, Celestial Craftsman.

Speak to us of the principles of the cosmos.

Prepare us that we may not be found wanting on the path of return.

Holy sub-lunar Architect,
Chief builder in creation,
To you we give praise. O holy
Artist, who opens ways none
May tread until it is time to

Return to the source, your ear
Do grant us. Strike with your hammer
  And let sparks loose in the sphere.

For creation is yours to rule
  And shape, and souls yours to free
Back into their spherical rounds.
  Holy Craftsman, hear our plea
And for the long journey home do
  fortify us. For our work
Is complete and heaven's labour
  Is a gift we would not shirk.

Holy King and Craftsman, you who fortifies the cosmos with your skilful art, we pray to you.
Daimon of Renowned Craft, who forged life from red clay, your names give sustenance to all who hear them.
In the beginning the world was forged, you work endlessly to complete it in accordance with Eternity.
The torrent of reason-principles fills the cosmos, you set them in their proper place.
Before your craftsmanship order had no voice, your skill sings lightning's song in the world.
There is none who can withstand the might of your work, or the beauty of your skill; all creation is completed
  through you.
Open our minds so we may contemplate the architecture of the cosmos and the harmony of your hand.
Protect us from division within our souls; separate the divine words into their proper places.
Each turn in our orbit brings us closer to your work, grant us the art to aid you in your governance.

Blessed Craftsman, who is skilled in
  Every art, we sing to you.
For you rectify every soul
  Incarnate according to
Divine principles. And through your
  Craft you mend false divisions

And you separate Sameness from
  Difference with your actions.

So hear this prayer, Many-Skilled Lord
  And aid us in completing
Our work in creation so we
  May travel on high and wing
Our way home. Lift our eyes to the
  Form of Beauty that even
Here shines with unseen glory; let
  Us return to what's been won.

Hear this prayer, O great King of Many Crafts, and be near us.
Lord of Inventions, who completes the work of creation with holy ingenuity, give ear.
Triumphant over matter, mighty smith and forger of the earthly realm, your actions bring all to fulfilling
  happiness.
Glorying in your work, the blows of your hammer shakes the cosmos into its proper place.
To some are given beauty and grace, your hand is grim, but your work shines with the light of the Form of
  Beauty.
Setting your mind on creation, your anvil rings with Form and life.
Let your insight into the Forms be granted to us that we may fulfil our divine ends.
Let your hand guide us as we proceed to the work of the Craftsman.
Through your many crafts, let us each find one appropriate to our soul.

The Evensong Prayer

Chariot-rejecting Craftsman, who rides into glory on a donkey's back, hear our prayers.
Great worker upon the stuff of creation, Bronze-Smith, Copper-Smith, Divine Craftsman, our orbits glorify your
  names.
The song of your anvil rings through the cosmos, O forger of peerless ingenuity.
In the bowels of the world you work tirelessly to fulfil the plans of the Celestial King.

For you rule the fiery depths and prove the worth of every soul.
The work of your hands brings safety to the cosmos, the righting of order over dissolution.
In your stillness the ring of your hammer vibrates through creation, let this harmony guide us on the return home.
In the depths of your forge you bring about beauty and life, let our work be a testament to your brilliance.
As you work to perfect the cosmos, let our souls be perfected as well.

Readings for Lectio Divina

[H]e infallibly and expertly brings to perfection each thing in accordance with truth… – Iamblichus, *De Mysteriis*, VIII.3.263.9-10.

For he is an image-maker and purifier of souls, always separating them from contrary reason-principles… – Iamblichus, *In Soph*, fr. I.2-4.

He fixes his gaze… on Real Being. – Iamblichus, *In Soph*, fr. I.7.

The Art of Division, again, imitates the procession of entities from the One, as does the Demiurge who presides over generation… - Iamblichus, *In Soph*, fr. I.14-16.

PRAYER SERVICE FOR THE MONTH OF AGROTEREION

The Hour of Dew Prayer

Most holy Lady, Queen of the Hunt, listen to our prayer.

Great Lady of lakes and broad pastures, whose pursuit none can escape, heed us.

O divine Maiden, Leader of the Dance, be near us.

From you comes life and death, the crescent moon strikes your darts into any who would trespass your virtue.

Your swift feet bring you to your prey, your dance ends in death and life.

For you are the Queen of the Chase, who drives her quarry along the path to their destiny.

You who are surrounded by virtue, help our souls be clean and pure that we may return home.

You who haunts the evening, lead us into the Celestial Light.

You whose arrows strike without fail, aim us deftly at our source.

The Noontide Prayers and Hymns

Divine Priestess and Far-shooting Queen, hear our prayer.

True Huntress and Companion of Virtue, hear our cry, O Lady of the Golden Arrows and life-raising Voice.

Ruler of the wild places where none but the purified may tread, Lady of Good Repute, be propitious.

The dart from your hand flies without erring, its strike sustains life.

The wild prey never escapes your gaze, your hand is forever without fault.

The strength of your voice brings life to the dead so that even those who fall in matter can gain heavenly immortality.

Grant us a clear vision of our path, that we may fly without erring to our source.

Speak to us of the wisdom of the hunt, that we may not be led astray.

Prepare us so we may ascend to the starry sky.

Hail to you, Nocturne's Light, Priestess
* Divine, Lady of sweet Hymns,*
Listen to our song. You whose dart
* Travels swiftly and so skims*
Through the air to its target, hear
* Us and be near. For your*
Straight aim is never-failing and
* You provide for our soul's cure.*

Artemis

Saviour of souls, Light-Bringer, take
  Us in hand, like your sacred
Arrows and fire us into
  The heavens, not earth-thick mud,
That we swiftly fly on noble
  Steeds to our source. Sacrosanct
Lady, Queen of divine fields, send
  Us back to where we are ranked.

Holy Queen and Consort of Virtue, you who oversee the bringing of new life into the divine realm, we pray to
  you.
Daimon of the Hymns, you who sing life into the world through your red art, your names give sustenance to all
  who hear them.
In the beginning you tricked disorder into its own doom, that generation may never overtake the heavens.
The torrent of heavenly arrows descend from your graceful hand, you slay the unvirtuous that they may be born
  again into the world for the sake of purification.
Before your fury none are safe, those who would violate heaven's virtue must face you.
There is none who matches your excellence or soothes souls like you.
Open the way before us, that none may be tripped by root or branch as we seek to travel home.
Protect us from our own unvirtuous folly.
Each turn in our orbit makes us wiser in your art, through you that which we pursue will be attained.

Holy Maiden, of chastity
  Pure, we praise you with this hymn
Of worship. Cunning Huntress, Queen
  Of wild places, our grim
Fate is yours to overturn as
  We seek the embrace of sweet
Providence. Make our virtue pure
  While on our chariot's seat.

For we would fly swiftly into
   The evening with your great light
To guide the way. Let your golden
   Darts slay within us the blight
Of impurity. Your arrows
   Burn the impure and give life
To those who seek your guidance. Let
   Them take us where there's no strife.

Hear this prayer, O great Queen who gives light to the evening darkness, and be near us.

Lady of the Wilderness, where no human treads, give ear.

Triumphant over impurity, mighty Huntress who helps souls being reborn into the divine realms, your actions
   bring all to fulfilling happiness.

Glorying in your chastity, your companions are the pure and virtuous.

To some are given the activity of purification, you raise up those who embrace them.

Setting your aim upon your prey, you release a golden shaft that only the virtuous may follow.

Let your song soothe us and your hymns perfect us.

Let the purity of our souls be like your arrows, sending us swiftly on our noble return.

Through your knowledge of the hunt, let our quarry, that holy daimon, never be out of sight.

The Evensong Prayer

Chariot-hunting Maiden, who sweeps through the forest on the backs of boar and deer and wolf, hear our prayer.

Great champion of the virtuous, Light-Bringer, those who haunt the wild places beyond humanity's reach, our
   orbits glorify your names.

The song of your lips soothes all who hear it, O Royal Priestess.

In the heart of the wilderness your arrows seek out those with impurity in their hearts.

For you rule the silvery orb, that holy reflection, by which souls are seen naked.

The bow and the spear you use to prove the virtue of those in your care.

In your stillness we see reflected the glory of the Celestial Creator.

In the cry of your voice we hear the way to our salvation.

As you hunt unseen paths, help us to make our way home.

Readings for Lectio Divina

Causing a rising up through the anagogic life. – *Chaldean Oracles*, fr. 123.4.

For the "warm breath" is the sharing of life. – *Chaldean Oracles*, fr. 123.4-5.

Why is it upon the mixed life that the Cause bestows itself? – Iamblichus, *In Phil*, fr. 6.1.

The purpose, then, of Hierarchy is the assimilation and union, as far as attainable, with God…
– Dionysius the Areopagite, *On the Heavenly Hierarchy*, I.2.

Hermes

PRAYER SERVICE FOR THE MONTH OF DIAKTOROSION

The Hour of Dew Prayer

Most holy Lord, divine tongue, source of speech, listen to our prayer.

Great and thoughtful King, who travels Necessity's dark path, heed us.

O divine Messenger, who gives the gift of prophecy and translates the divine will to mortal kin, be near us.

From you true words spring from mortal lips and by your hand are the dead led to their fate.

Your Word harmonizes the divine elements within all who hear it, your decree is the Word of the Creator.

For you know the divine ways, and your ingenuity discerns the pure from the impure.

You who know the pathways to heaven, guide us towards our home.

You who harmonize the similar and dissimilar, grant harmony to our souls.

You whose art transcends human understanding, let our minds be filled with you.

The Noontide Prayers and Hymns

Divine Lord of Rebirth and chief Minister, hear our prayer.

True Messenger of the Seven-Rayed Lord, hear our cry, O Heart-Delighting Child.

Ruler of the paths between heaven and earth, Friend of those who search for harmonious wisdom, be propitious.

The staff of your office reconciles all opposites; peace comes to wherever you travel.

The flocks which you protect never become lost; you rescue all in peril.

The strength of your arm slays a hundred watchful foes, none may hinder you in your task.

Grant us the knowledge of the heavenly roads that we might find our ways home.

Speak to us the names of our heavenly guardians.

Prepare us that we may welcome the one set over us with wisdom and grace.

Keeper of the Flocks of souls in
*   Their orbits, O Divine Word*
Of the Seven-Rayed King, please hear
*   Our song to you. Like a bird*
You flit between heaven and Earth
*   And even Death's gate cannot*

Bar you from your appointed work;
   Your great Word may not be fought.

True Speech of God, Voice heard throughout
   The world, hear us, recorder
Of virtue and fault. Grant us your
   Knowledge so we do not slur
Our souls' truth. Grant us peace, balance,
   And great cunning that wisdom
Falls from our lips and guides our feet
   As we dance to your pipe's thrum.

Holy Keeper of Flocks, Soul of Becoming, we pray to you.
Daimon of True Speech, you who are the Voice of that which will come to pass, your names give sustenance to
   all who hear them.
In the Beginning the Celestial Majesty Spoke, and you were the Word of Creation.
The torrent of falsehood drowns the moral realm, but you separate knowledge from opinion.
Before your guidance, souls lose themselves in Necessity's embrace; you lead souls to their proper place.
There is none who may hinder your passage in this realm or the next.
Open our mouths that your wisdom may spill from them.
Protect us from internal strife which may prevent us from returning home.
Each turn in our orbits leads us closer to you, you who know the names of our daimons.

Champion of divine games, Lord
   Of all Words, we sing your praise
And call to you, O Immortal
   Guide of returning souls. Blaze
Your trail before us and let us
   Not be lost to Death's embrace
But instead raise us to heaven's
   Summit and our proper place.

For you, O soul's harmony and
  Guide, speak to our souls divine
Truth and fill the heavens with peace.
  Help us to quicken our pace
As we journey upwards. Fill us
  With your vast and pure knowledge
That we may separate truth from
  Belief and cross heaven's bridge.

Hear this prayer, O great King and Reconciler of Opposites, and be near us.
Lord of the Divine Word, who knows all the divine names, give ear.
Triumphant over the cosmos, you who see Eternity and from whom nothing is hidden, your actions bring all to
  fulfilling happiness.
Glorying in your journey, your attendants range over field and forest, seeking throughout the whole of the world.
To some are given fleetness of tongue, but to you comes both deftness and hidden truth.
Setting your sword in hand, you cleave opinion from knowledge.
Let your mind enumerate the stars to us, that we may be directed toward our own.
Let your mighty speech inspire us, you who are the heart of the Divine Mind.
Through your Truth and Righteousness, may the divine words be resonant within us.

The Evensong Prayer

Chariot-steering Messenger of the Blessed Ones, who goes wherever providence dictates, hear our prayer.
Great Champion, whose visage sets the boundaries between realms, our orbits glorify your names.
The songs of your travels fill mortals and immortals alike with wonder, O Lord of Necessity's paths.
In the heavens you receive the divine command, you travel all the cosmoses to fulfil your duty.
For you rule the golden herds and allow none to be lost in the darkness.
The pipes and the pen, the tools of your trades, lead souls to their proper places.
In your stillness let us find the answers to every question, for your knowledge is unending.
In the quest of each of our souls, lead us to victory.
As you return to the celestial abode, take us with you to the heavenly summit.

Readings for Lectio Divina

Hermes, the god who presides over rational discourse, has long been considered, quite rightly, to be the common patron of all priests; he who presides over true knowledge about the gods is one and the same always and everywhere. – Iamblichus, *De Mysteriis*, I.1.1.1-2.2.

The Stranger should be conceived in the role of the Father of the Demiurges, being supercelestial and transcendent, and his hearers as the demiurgic thoughts, the one in the role of the thought of Zeus, the other in the role of a messenger, as being Hermaic and a geometer. – Iamblichus, *In Soph.*, fr. I.18-21.

Wherefore, beyond all, they are deemed pre-eminently worthy of the appellation Angelic, on the ground that the supremely Divine illumination comes to them at first hand, and, through them, there pass to us manifestations above us. – Pseudo-Dionysius, *The Celestial Hierarchy*, IV.2.180B.

The theologians also call the most holy ranks of the highest Beings "Angels," for they also make known the supremely Divine illumination. – Pseudo-Dionysius, *The Celestial Hierarchy*, V.I196C.

PRAYER SERVICE FOR THE MONTH OF KHRYSOPÊLÊXION

The Hour of Dew Prayer

Most holy Lord, saviour of cities and ally of Justice, listen to our prayer.
Great warrior who governs the rebellious soul, heed us.
O divine warrior and protector, Golden-helmed King, be near us.
From you comes deadly shafts to pierce the poisonous chiton which impedes the divine chariots.
Your might stops chaos from upsetting the divine realm, your fiery chariot warns all of your purpose.
For you hurl the golden spears and wield a mighty blade and beneath you Justice's foes are sundered.
You who are brave of heart and mighty of will, bolster us as we near our destination.
You who are the balance of beauty's harmony, let the scales of our hearts and minds not be unbalanced.
You who punish those who strive against Justice's vision, give us the strength to offer ourselves to unyielding
    providence.

The Noontide Prayers and Hymns

Divine Chariot-Rider, mighty in strength, silver-armed and golden-helmed, hear our prayer.
True Guardian of the celestial skies, hear our cry, O unwearying protector of heaven.
Ruler of the third sphere, who protects the final path to heaven, be propitious.
The shield of your strong arm protects the righteous and the innocent against harm from the defilement of the stuff
    of generation.
The bright flame of your unsheathed sword strikes down all who oppose heavenly dispensation.
The cry of your lips brings courage to all who hear it.
Grant us victory over temptation and cowardice of heart.
Speak to us of triumph over the profane that we may redeem it for the divine purpose.
Prepare us that we may not be taken unawares by foes without or within.

Heaven's Warrior, golden-helmed
   And brazen-armed, hear us. Lord
Of the fiery sphere, whose blade does
   Blind Heaven's foes, let your sword
Strike down the foes of virtue and
   Save all the souls who would seek

Ares

To return home by just decree;
   Protect us, we who are weak.

O Heaven's Defender, Lord of
   Hosts, Justice's Friend, ally
To the righteous, you bring low the
   Foes of virtue and your sigh
Hastens impurity's fall. Grant
   Us all courage in the face
Of that darkly splendid world and
   Protect for us Heaven's grace.

Holy Defender of the heavenly hosts, leader of the righteous, we pray to you.

Daimon of victory through contest, you who stay rage and strife, your names give sustenance to all who hear them.

In the Beginning you defended the divine kingdom, now you guard our way back home.

The torrent of spears and arrows rain down upon the mortal realm, your holy ray gives courage even in the face of
   death.

Before your onslaught those who revel in cruelty and delight in impurity fall to Necessity's dire lesson.

There is none who matches your indomitable will or dauntless courage.

Open the gate to our heavenly home that we may enter and stand before our source.

Protect us from the arrows of spite and hubris that we may be clean before the holy countenance.

Each turn in our orbits readies us and wearies us, we are ready to return home and take up our appointed tasks,
   let us enter and rejoice.

You who rallies souls in their course,
   Stayer of rage, Champion
Of righteousness and justice, hear
   Our prayer. Set your beacon
In the night so it may guide us
   To safe harbour. Rain spears

Upon Justice's foes and grant
  Us courage against cruel jeers.

O King of battles, silver-armed
  And full of righteousness, gift
Respite to our journey and ward
  Our way with your blade that's swift.
Triumphant one, King of Courage,
  Ward our passage with your shield
And protect each returning soul
  So they have no cause to yield.

Hear this prayer, O great King and battle-hardened protector, and be near us.
Lord of hard-fought battles, who gives respite to the war-weary, give ear.
Triumphant over cowardice, divine guardian of the celestial pathways, your actions bring all to fulfilling happiness.
Glorying in your courage, fear and terror are in your train, for they are yours to command.
To some are given strength of heart and mind, their bravery stems from your providence.
Setting your wards in place, where you stand fear and defeat may not enter.
Let your arm protect our journey as we at last approach our homes.
Let your shield guard us from all harm.
Through your strong spirit let us have courage to stand before our source and be not afraid.

The Evensong Prayer

Chariot-driving warrior, whose vehicle is drawn by flaming steeds, hear our prayer.
Great protector, warrior of justice and honour, our orbits glorify your names.
The songs of your battles fill all who hear them with bravery and honour, O you who rallies the righteous
  defender.
In the heat of battle you let neither fear nor chaos loose; they are always in your command.
For your hand bound the night's terror, and your wrath strikes down all threats to divine temperance.
The sword you use to protect all who live with pious intent.

In your stillness we find the bravery of our souls to stand for what is right.
In the honour of your Word we find the strength to live the truths of our souls.
As you defend the battle-weary defend us, for our hard journey is over and we would rest from our challenges.

Readings for Lectio Divina

Stay the rage, stay the strife, relax pain's grip on my soul. – Orphic Hymns, *To Ares*, 6.

Shed down a kindly ray from above upon my life, and strength of war, that I may be able to drive away bitter cowardice from my head and crush down the deceitful impulses of my soul. – Homeric Hymns, *To Ares*.

Brave…we call each individual by virtue of this part in him, when, namely, his high spirit preserves in the midst of pains and pleasures the rule handed down by the reason as to what is or is not to be feared. – Plato, *Republic*, IV.442c.

Arrayed from head to toe with clamorous light, armed in mind and soul with a triple-barbed strength, you must cast into your imagination the entire token of the triad, and not go toward the empyrean channels in a scattered way, but with concentration. – *Chaldean Oracles*, fr. 2.1-4.

Haides

PRAYER SERVICE FOR THE MONTH OF NEKRODEGMÔNION

The Hour of Dew Prayer

Most holy Lord, saviour of the innumerable dead, listen to our prayer.

Great Queen of initiates, master of daimons, whose realm touches all places and nowhere, heed us.

O divine one, three-fold unity who leads us to the places in between life and death, the sacred and profane, be near us.

From you the mysteries of life and death are revealed to the worthy, you Ruler of Many; initiates and their guardians alike.

Your wisdom judges all deeds, obscure and conspicuous, for the roads and crossroads are yours,
* In the heavens and beneath the earth you see the secrets of every soul.*

For you see in the hearts of every initiate, and all those who seek divine wisdom, your torch illuminates the depths.

You who hold the knowledge of the Divine Mind in your heart, favour us with divine insight and the names of our daimons.

You who rule the Earth and beneath it, our journey begins and ends with you, let us enter the hall of death that is initiation.

You whose heart is tender with justice and moderation, make our hearts like those who are drunk with innocence and divine providence.

The Noontide Prayers and Hymns

Divine King of Hosts, saviour of the whole world, hear our prayer.

True Saviour of the Dead and Initiates alike, hear our cry, O giver of wealth.

Ruler of Daimons, dire judge of necessity's calling, be propitious.

The sceptre in your hand commands every spirit of the twelve-fold heavens.

The keys which set our divine guardians to their ordained wards only you command.

The fruit of your kingdom raises the quick and traps the dead.

Grant us the names of our allotted daimons that we may be truly guided.

Speak to us of the laws of Necessity that they may be overcome.

Prepare us so we not become mired in your sense-dulling kingdom but travel our route in safety and wisdom.

Great King of Souls, divine saviour

To whom all at last do fall,
Hear our prayer. Lord of Daimons,
  Judge of souls, to your dire hall
All must travel, and you assess
  Their waste and their great riches
Before setting them back on course.
  Hear this song of the ages.

Holy initiator, Queen
  Of by-ways, darkness' Lord
And wheel-spinner, who sets souls to
  Live and die, above the horde
Do set us and your mysteries
  Reveal. Send us our divine
Guides. Let our providence be won
  By holy rites which are thine.

Holy maker of initiates, Saviour and Sorceress, we pray to you.
Daimon of the night, King who receives many, Lady of the Underworld, your names give sustenance to all who
    hear them.
In the Beginning your lot fell to the third realm, and so, with your triple flame and sacred wheel,
You guide and judge the souls of your place, some you keep, some release, initiated into your divine mysteries.
The torrent of daimons flows from your realm into ours, travelling the four-fold path.
Before your Word is spoken, all of daimon-kind seeks to obey your command, your sceptre releases them from
    below and returns them again.
There are none like you, O many-headed Creator, for you see all the world and no secret, mortal or divine, is
    hidden from you.
Open your realm and release to us our daimons.
Protect us from the mire of generation with your charms and sacred incantations.
Each turn in our orbits brings us to you; release us so we may continue on our sacred voyage.
Maidenly Queen and Sorceress,

Master of Earth-bound souls, we
Sing to you, O many-headed
* Mistress. Give to us the key*
To your kingdom, let us open
* The gate behind which daimons*
Dwell, and now protect us from the
* Dross of all that goodness shuns.*

Night's Wandering Lady, Divine
* Maiden and image-maker*
Through your mysteries, our triumph
* Over death is like armour*
For our souls. You rejuvenate
* Those within your care, revive*
Us to heavenly life so that
* In our orbits we may thrive.*

Hear this prayer, O great Queen and divine image-maker, and be near us.
Lady of the Night, who awaits us at the wayside, give ear.
Triumphant over death, nurse of those made young by the mysteries, your actions bring all to fulfilling happiness.
Glorying in your triple light, half of you is exposed to the wise, and half of you is known only to the dead.
To some are given a life of bondage to Necessity, your kiss gives release into providence's embrace.
Setting your torches in place you see the whole of the world and the depths of every soul.
Let your nighttime wandering lead you to us that we may be awake before dawn.
Let your sacred names liberate us from ignorance.
Through your mysteries let us once more rise to the celestial sun.

The Evensong Prayer

Chariot-mounted King, whose deathly steeds steal away in the night, hear our prayer.
Great and only-begotten maiden, our orbits glorify your names.

The songs of your daimons call out to those within their series, O great Queen of those below.
In the maze of generation you receive the lost and those guided by higher purpose, some you keep and others you
   set free.
For your command releases souls in bondage to Necessity and your key unlocks the darkest gate.
The triple-brilliance of your sacred form beguiles the impure and illuminates the initiate.
In your stillness we know the silence of sacred Death, the last mystery our mortal eyes may see.
In the comfort of your realm those ignorant of their essence learn the truth of their nature, let
Your mysteries grant us this knowledge before we lie down to sleep.
As you return to your dark abode, leave open to us heavenly passages.

Readings for Lectio Divina

When a man dies, his own guardian spirit, which was given charge over him in his life, tries to bring him to a certain place where all must assemble, and from which, after submitting their several cases to judgment, they must set out for the next world, under the guidance of one who has the office of escorting souls from this world to the other. – Plato, *Phaedo*, 107d-e.

For you must not gaze at them until you have your body initiated. – *Chaldean Oracles*, fr. 135.3-4.

For the theurgists do not fall into the herd which is subject to Destiny. – *Chaldean Oracles*, fr 153.3.

The telestic life contributes the most by removing, through divine fire, all the 'defilements' attendant upon generation… – *Chaldean Oracles*, fr. 196.1-2.

Bibliography

Anastos, Milton V. 'Pletho's Calendar and Liturgy.' *Dumbarton Oaks Papers* 4 (1948): 183-305.

Athanassakis, Apostolos N. and Wolkow, Benjamin M., translators. *The Orphic Hymns.* Baltimore, MD: Johns Hopkins University Press, 2013.

Betz, Hans Dieter. 'The Delphic Maxim "Know Yourself" in the PGM.' *History of Religions* 2.2 (1981): 156-171.

Copenhaver, Brian P. 'Hermes Trismegistus, Proclus, and the Question of a Philosophy of Magic in the Renaissance.' In *Hermeticism and the Renaissance*, edited by Ingrid Merkel and Allen G. Debus, 79-110. Washington, D.C.: Folger Books, 1988.

Cross, Tom Peete and Slover, Clark Harris, editors. *Ancient Irish Tales.* NY: Barnes & Noble Books, 1996.

Evelyn-White, Huge G., translator. *Hesiod, Homeric Hymns, and Homerica.* Cambridge: Harvard University Press, 1914.

Gandz, Solomon. 'The Calendar-Reform of Pletho (c. 1355 – c. 1450): Its Significance and Its Place in the History of the Calendar.' *Osiris* 9 (1950): 199-210.

Gilman, Ken. 'Twelve Gods and Seven Planets.' Last viewed 3/16/15. http://cura.free.fr/decem/10kengil.html

Hamilton, Edith. Mythology: Timeless Tales of Gods and Heroes. NY: Warner Books, 1969.

'HMEPA: Hellenic Month Established Per Athens.' Last viewed 3/16/15. http://www.numachi.com/~ccount/hmepa/

Iamblichus. *De Anima: Text, Translation, and Commentary.* Translated by John F. Finamore and John M. Dillon. Atlanta: Society of Biblical Literature, 2002.

—. *De Mysteriis.* Translated by Emma C. Clarke, John M. Dillon and Jackson P. Hershbell. Atlanta. GA: Society of Biblical Literature, 2003.

—. *In Platonis Dialogos Commentariorum Fragmenta.* Translated by Dillon, John M. Wiltshire, UK: Prometheus Trust, 2009.

—. *The Letters.* Translated by John M. Dillon and Wolfgang Polleichtner. Atlanta, GA: Society of Biblical Literature, 2009.

Julianus the Theurgist. *The Chaldean Oracles: Text, Translation, and Commentary.* Translated by Majercik, Ruth Dorothy. Leiden, The Netherlands: Brill, 1989.

Kupperman, Jeffrey. *Living Theurgy*, London: Avalonia Books, 2014.

—. 'Where the Goddess and God Walk: An Examination of Myth and Ritual in Revivalist Pagan Sabbat Celebrations with Particular Reference to the Temple of the Sacred Craft.' PhD diss, University of Liverpool, 2007.

Nicolaidis, Efthymios. *Science and Eastern Orthodoxy.* Baltimore, MD: Johns Hopkins University Press, 2011.

Pieraccini, Lisa C. *Around the Hearth: Caeretan Cylinder-Stamped Braziers.* Rome: «L'ERMA» de BRETSCHNEIDER, 2003.

Plato. *Collected Dialogues.* Edited by Edith Hamilton and Huntington Cairns. Princeton: Princeton University Press, 1980.

—. *The Dialogues of Plato, in 5 vols.* Translated by Benjamin Jowett. London: Oxford University Press, 1892.

Proclus. *Elements of Theology.* Translated by E. R. Dodds. Oxford: Clarendon Press, 1963.

—. *Hymns: Essays, Translations, Commentary.* Translated by Van Den Berg, R. M. Leiden, The Netherlands: Brill, 2001.

Pseudo-Dionysius. *The Works of Dionysius the Areopagite.* Translated by John Parker. Veritatis Splendour Publications, 2013.

Regardie, Israel. *The Golden Dawn.* St. Paul, MN: Llewellyn Publications, 1993.

Sallustius. *Concerning the Gods and the Universe.* Translated by Arthur Darby Nock. Chicago: Ares Publishers, Inc., 1926.

Shaw, Gregory. 'The Geometry of Grace: A Pythagorean Approach to Theurgy.' In *The Divine Iamblichus: Philosopher and Man of Gods*, edited by H.J. Blumenthal and E.G. Clark, 117-137. London: Bristol classical Press, 1993.

Simeoni, Manuela, trans. 'Hymns to the Gods by George Gemistos Plethon.' Last viewed 2/27/15. http://www.giornopaganomemoria.it/plethonhymns.html.

Sturluson, Snorri. *Edda.* NY: Everyman's Library, 1995.

Temperance, 'Solstices.' Last viewed 3/16/15 http://baringtheaegis.blogspot.com/2013/08/solstices-and-calculations-on-hellenic.html.

Terry, Patricia, translator. *Poems of the Elder Edda.* Philadelphia, University of Pennsylvania Press, 1990.

Uždavinys, Algis. *Philosophy and Theurgy in Late Antiquity*, San Rafael, CA: Angelico Press, 2010.

Index

www.avaloniabooks.com

CPSIA information can be obtained
at www.ICGtesting.com
Printed in the USA
LVHW010045140721
692557LV00005B/196

9 781905 297894